MW01110050

Come and step into a [...]
oil of joy for mournin[...]
spirit of heaviness (Isai[...]

Give me thirty days of your attention and you can step into a journey that will change the way you think—not just about life, but about you. When you change the way you think and feel about yourself, your life changes.

That is what you will experience after reading *Step into the Beauty of Holiness*. This book will lead you on a journey to cleanse your mind, your spirit, and your emotions of the past.

By reading the daily devotionals and answering some of the thought-provoking questions, this book will guide you through life's deepest and toughest questions: why did all this happen to me and how can it be used? Well, if you are ready to do the work, you will reap the harvest of stepping into a brand-new day. Your life may have once been riddled with pain and shame, but it can now be filled with glory and gain. Enjoy the journey as you step into the beauty of wholeness.

—Bishop Al & Pastor Tee Way
Ecclesiastical Covering Ministry, Faith Assembly of Christ, Washington, D.C.

Holiness has never gone out of style and it never will. It is the foundation of true beauty, for it contains within it integrity, honor, and truth! Developing inner beauty is the aim of every believer. Allowing the fruit of the Spirit to develop in our lives is a lifelong process assisted by the Holy Spirit. These daily devotions will assist with that process of development and transformation.

In this book, Evangelist Pressey addresses the entire individual—spirit, soul, and body. She acknowledges the triune nature of mankind and prescribes strategies for self-care.

Building a life of devotion will increase the consistency we need to be victorious! Thanks to Evangelist Pressey, there is another tool available for women to assist them in becoming holy before the Lord!

—Dr. Karen S. Bethea, Senior Pastor
Set the Captives Free Outreach Center, Windsor Mill, Maryland

While this devotional appears to be primarily directed toward women, I found many of the daily topics to be helpful for anyone seeking to reaffirm, rededicate, reset, or even begin a relationship not only with the Lord but with themselves and everyone they may come in contact with. The devotionals are plain, easy-to-understand concepts—many that we are already familiar with or have heard in cliché ways throughout our life's journey.

This book takes what is familiar and guides us to a deeper understanding of what we think we know and inserts truth in a non-threatening, spirit-invoking way that is further solidified in our minds and hearts by the requirement to identify action steps which help us put to our rejuvenated thoughts into actions to make that life change.

Even more refreshing are the personal accounts of challenges the author has experienced and successfully been able to navigate on her way back to a spiritually healthy relationship with herself and the Lord. Now she is paying it forward by helping us do the same. Enjoy the journey and be blessed!

—Pamela D. Jenkins
First Baptist Church of Glenarden, Bowie, Maryland

This devotional is a testimony of God's persistent steadfast love and faithfulness, revealed in my sister's life. This precious soul, Jacqueline Pressey, has known suffering from her infancy, having contracted spinal meningitis at five months old and miraculously recovered. God's hand has been on her life ever since.

Though Jacqueline's lupus was not diagnosed until early adulthood, it provided the family with an explanation for her previous years of multiple symptoms. Jacqueline learned to trust God in the midst of her affliction. When the reader engages this material, not only will they benefit from the skilled instruction of a professor, they will fellowship with her in her sufferings and learn to apply God's word in their own trials.

In her brokenness, Jacqueline chose to focus on Jesus and testify to his goodness to others. Over the years she has been resilient in avoiding bitterness in her trials, but instead welcomed the forging of Christ-likeness. I believe this is her hope for the women who will be helped. With great joy, I recommend this devotional, *Step into the Beauty of Holiness*.

—Sandra D. Walton
Children's Ministry Teacher, Sovereign Grace Church, Woodstock, Georgia

Dear reader, I would like to introduce you to my mom. She is blessed. I knew at an early age that her perspective has always been unique. I know that she has been specially chosen by God and has been set apart for a royal destiny.

She's a warrior, gentle but strong, sensitive, diligent, consistent, and faithful. She loves excitedly, is lots of fun, and might I add she's hilarious! She's a mama bear for sure, a protector, uncompromising with her relationship with God, and an overcomer. She's bold and multifaceted, and through relationship with God invites all those who cross her path to experience Him. My mom is truly a visionary and a shining example of a Proverbs 31 woman.

As you begin your journey through this book, it is my prayer that you will be whole. May God reveal Himself to you in a brand new way through each daily devotion. Blessings to you!

—Jacquelynn Pressey

FCSG Sister,
Pastor Tia Coutroupis

You were my 1st purchase
from FCSG 9/16/17
Thank you!

Step INTO THE Beauty OF Holiness

Evanglist Jacquelin M Bossy
A Facilitator
of Inspiration

Jan
2018

A 30 Day Devotional for Women

Step INTO THE Beauty OF Holiness

JACQUELINE M. PRESSEY
EVANGELIST/HOSPITAL CHAPLAIN

Printed in Canada

ISBN: 978-1-4866-1460-8

Word Alive Press
131 Cordite Road, Winnipeg, MB R3W 1S1
www.wordalivepress.ca

Library and Archives Canada Cataloguing in Publication

Pressey, Jacqueline M., author
    Step into the beauty of holiness / Jacqueline M. Pressey.

ISBN 978-1-4866-1460-8 (softcover)

    1. Devotional exercises. 2. Devotional literature. 3. Devotion.
I. Title.

BV4832.3.P74 2017   242   C2017-901482-X

TABLE OF CONTENTS

INTRODUCTION

Follow peace with all men, and holiness,
without which no man shall see the Lord…
(Hebrews 12:14)

[I]t is actually impossible for someone to dwell in God's presence without being holy. That's why holy living is a big deal!

When we talk about the subject of holiness, it's essential we understand it is not about control, guilt, or adherence to a man-made standard. It's about relationship.[1]

John Bevere has suggested that we must each pursue our own holiness through developing a godly lifestyle. One needs to first become a student of God's Word, and second to be attentive to God's Spirit growing in your life.

Step into the Beauty of Holiness has been purposefully written with you in mind. This devotional presents specific topics that focus on common areas of the struggle between the mind, flesh, and the spirit. As you journey toward the beauty of holiness, you will access and self-examine your mind, heart, emotions, motives, soul/spirit, and body.

It is my sincere desire and prayer that this book will assist you in becoming whole and comfortable in the uniqueness in which God has made you, to become the authentic you through our Lord Jesus Christ.

Let me introduce myself. I am Jacqueline M. Pressey, an evangelist, hospital chaplain, and the founder of Recreations Ministries in White

---

1 John Bevere, *Messenger International*, "The Two Things We Need to Do Holiness Well." Date of access: April 1, 2017 (http://messengerinternational.org/blog/devotional/the-two-things-we-need-to-do-holiness-well).

Plains, Maryland. As part of my service to the community, I established a ministry and foundation called Operation Rescue.[2] I completed my Hospital Chaplaincy level 1 clinicals in pastoral care education program at Georgetown University Hospital in Washington D.C. where I continue to serve as a hospital chaplain.

Basically, I am a servant/transformational leader who lives to inspire and make a difference in the lives of others in my community, society, and the world. This devotional writing project began in 2003. I thought at the time that I wanted to share insights that would assist women in stepping into the beauty of holiness in their own lives, based on this foundational scripture: *"Give unto the Lord the glory due unto his name: bring an offering, and come before him: worship the Lord in the beauty of holiness"* (1 Chronicles 16:29). I never thought in a million years that it would take fourteen years before the Lord pushed me to publish it.

Throughout my fifty-six years of life, I have been a daughter, a sister, a wife of thirty-one years, a mother of three children, a pastor/minister's wife for over twenty years, an academic professor/advisor, a mentor and student for twenty-five years, a friend, a woman of God, divorced after thirty-one years of marriage, and a happily single woman serving God with my whole heart for more than seven years.

So what happened? In 2003, I had this great idea to write a book that would give the reader guidance, short assignments, and prayer projects that would lead them into the beauty of holiness. But before I could ever tell anyone how to get there, the Lord wanted to lead me there first. It has taken me approximately twelve years to develop a lifestyle that is founded on the Word of God, empowering me to inspire others to seek the beauty of holiness. Now, after my fifteen-year journey towards attaining a life

---

2 Operation Rescue is a non-profit outreach ministry with a global view. Our services support others through providing food, shelter, and funds, focusing on assisting other in times of crises, homelessness, and medical emergencies in our local communities, society, and the world.

that radiates the beauty of holiness, I can share with you what I have learned through this ongoing process of growth.

Welcome to the journey of the death of yourself, or should I say the death of your flesh? You are the offering that God wants, but you have to give yourself away first. The only way the Lord can make you beautiful is through holiness, living a surrendered life, and allowing God to get all the glory.

What you will discover through this short book are nuggets and principles that will help you to become more beautiful in the sight of God. God's beauty is different from the outward beauty of the world. His vision of beauty comes from the innermost part of us—the mind, heart, and soul/spirit. He wants to make us beautiful, and He wants us to want to be beautiful in and through Him.

Are you ready to take the time and do the work that it will take to become beautiful through holiness? If the answer is yes, brace yourself and read on. If not, give this book away and bless someone who needs it and is ready to change. I will be praying for all of you who choose to step into the beauty of holiness with me. I love it here, even though it's a lifelong work in progress.

Scripture Foundation

Give unto the Lord the glory due unto his name: bring
an offering, and come before him: worship
the Lord in the beauty of holiness.
(1 Chronicles 16:29)

Give unto the Lord the glory due unto his name; worship
the Lord in the beauty of holiness.
(Psalm 29:2)

Wherefore gird up the loins of your mind, be sober, and
hope to the end for the grace that is to be brought unto
you at the revelation of Jesus Christ; as obedient children,
not fashioning yourselves according to the former lusts in
your ignorance: but as he which hath called you is holy,
so be ye holy in all manner of conversation; because
it is written, Be ye holy; for I am holy.
(1 Peter 1:13–16)

The Lord will perfect that which concerneth me: thy
mercy, O Lord, endureth for ever: forsake not
the works of thine own hands.
(Psalm 138:8)

DEVOTIONAL GUIDELINES

1. Before stepping into this journey, pray and be willing to commit to the thirty-day focus. Journey in secret and keep quiet about this until you have finished all thirty devotionals. Only share this journey with the accountability partner you select for this process.

> But thou, when thou prayest, enter into thy closet, and
> when thou hast shut thy door, pray to thy Father which is
> in secret; and thy Father which seeth in secret
> shall reward thee openly.
> (Matthew 6:6)

2. Designate a consistent time and place for your devotional assignments and reflections. Your assignments will take place at the end of each week.

Action Steps

Are any behavior changes that will provide the foundation for holiness improvements in your life? For example, say that you will stop complaining this week. If a complaint or negative thought comes to your mind about yourself or others, replace it with a prayer of thanksgiving.

3. Seek out a reliable accountability partner who will hold you accountable for the process and the work.

4. Prayer and reflection are key to developing lasting behavioral changes, so don't rush through the material, even if it takes you longer than a month.

5. Use more than one version of the Bible. This will assist you with in-depth study, and it will enrich your understanding of the Word of God.

6. The forgiveness process starts with self-examination. First go into prayer and forgive anyone who has injured you or whom you perceive has injured you, even if they are deceased. This journey into wholeness is about you, personally.

7. If you have not received Christ as your personal Savior, please make this your number one priority of the book: accept Jesus Christ as your Lord and Savior and give Him permission to guide you. The effectiveness of this holiness journey will depend on it.

On _____ (date),

I _____ (name),

agree to abide by the guidelines the author
has outlined for this devotional journey.

God bless you, and my prayers are with you. Come and join me on the other side of stepping into the beauty of holiness—and that is *living* in the beauty of holiness.

Prayer Commitment

- I agree to set aside at least one hour per day to pray for myself and the needs of others and my church.
- I agree to seek the Lord for guidance, healing, and help with living a beautiful life of holiness.
- I agree not to judge or be critical of others who don't understand, or who are not interested in, this journey that I am on toward stepping into the beauty of holiness.
- I agree to be led by the Lord, and I truly want to be used by the Lord and do what God has called me to do, no matter where I am in my life, walk with God, or my situations or issues.
- I agree to pass on this book to another as a gift, if it has encouraged me or blessed me in any way.
- I agree to lift the author, her family, and ministry up so that she can continue to make a difference in the lives of others and this world.

Signature: _____

Date: _____

Week One

BROKEN FOR YOU:
BEAUTY CARE FOR THE MIND

The sacrifices of God are a broken spirit:
a broken and a contrite heart,
O God, thou wilt not despise.
(Psalm 51:17)

DAY ONE

The Mindset

SCRIPTURE READING: 1 CHRONICLES 16:10–12

MEMORY VERSE
*Give unto the Lord the glory due unto his name: bring
an offering, and come before him: worship
the Lord in the beauty of holiness.*
(1 Chronicles 16:29)

Holiness. What is true holiness? It is "the state of being holy… [and] is defined by one being sound, happy, and whole… consecrated, sacred, pure and untainted by evil or sin… [Holiness] is demonstrated by a deep reverence, awe, respect and adoration for the Lord Jesus Christ."[3] The Word of God states,

*But as he which hath called you is holy, so be ye holy in
all manner of conversation; because it is written,
Be ye holy; for I am holy.*
(1 Peter 1:15–16)

---

[3] Jack Hayford, *Charisma Magazine*, "Jack Hayford Explains What Holiness Really Is." August 26, 2015 (http://www.charismamag.com/spirit/spiritual-growth/14575–wholly-holy).

Based on today's scripture text today, the process of being truly holy starts with us giving glory to the Savior's holy name. Second, we must have a heart that can rejoice in the Lord; third, we must be able to seek the Lord and ask for His guidance and strength continually. We must also have a mindset that is tuned to the principles of holy living.

Having worked with thousands of women through health, wellness, and fitness classes, many of them sought perfectionism and self-esteem through their outward appearance. Many were insecure, fearful of the aging process, and obsessed with trying to attract a man, fame, or fortune. Well, none of these will last. Having a worldly, external view of one's self-image is a clear road to disaster. And it breeds an enormous amount of stress and anxiety.

It is time to change your way of thinking and use the Word of God to fight the old mindset. By learning and applying principles of holiness, you can develop new mental and emotional patterns that will calm the spirit and empower the Lord to rule your life.

The first key to experiencing wholeness is to thank the Lord for ruling your life and for making you. You were fearfully and wonderfully made.

I will praise thee; for I am fearfully
and wonderfully made: marvellous are thy works;
and that my soul knoweth right well.
(Psalm 139:14)

God does not make mistakes, although you may need to improve spiritually, emotionally, and physically and trust the one who created you to help you. The next step is to ask the Lord to forgive you of any negative views and opinions you have mentally rehearsed in your mind. When you ask Him to cleanse your heart, you'll be able to present a heart that rejoices in the presence of the Lord. And finally, seek God's strength continually. Pray every step of the way! Seek His face in everything you do. Seek Him in every change you make. Seek Him! Seek Him! And seek Him some more!

Prayer Guide

Dear Heavenly Father, I am starting this journey to wholeness today, _____ (date). I honor and glorify You for making me. Your Word says that I am fearfully and wonderfully made. I received this revelation and I ask You to forgive me for any unrighteousness in my mind and heart. Please forgive me and cleanse my heart, making it a heart that daily rejoices in Your presence. I'm seeking your face in this endeavor; my trust will be in You. Give me the strength to discipline my mind, emotions, and flesh so that this vessel radiates the beauty of holiness. Lead me this day and forever, Amen!

Action Step:

DAY TWO

The Life of Thoughts

SCRIPTURE READING: 2 CORINTHIANS 3:1–18

MEMORY VERSE

*Now the Lord is that Spirit: and where the Spirit of
the Lord is, there is liberty. But we all, with open face
beholding as in a glass the glory of the Lord, are changed
into the same image from glory to glory,
even as by the Spirit of the Lord.*
(2 Corinthians 3:17–18)

What are you thinking? A person's thought life is one of the first
areas that must be disciplined. Thoughts give rise to emotions,
actions, and behaviors. For example, if in your mind you think that you
are insignificant, your body will carry out the accompanying actions. In
your demeanor, you may show signs of insecurity, low self-esteem, and
worthlessness.

Do you see how a simple thought can mold your destiny? By
addressing the inner man—the mind, heart, and emotions—you can
improve your outward actions. God's glory can only radiate from vessels
who possess the Spirit of the Lord on the inside. Through His Word, we
become living epistles to be seen and read by men (2 Corinthians 3:2).

Do a spiritual life checkup by answering this question: what is your life displaying and/or attracting?

Becoming a living epistle means becoming a living letter of God's Word and glory. Your thoughts can be disciplined, and even commanded to be subject, to the spirit of the Lord. By allowing the Spirit of the Lord to rule in your heart and mind, you will obtain liberty. Liberty means freedom from the oppressiveness of negative thoughts that have controlled your mind and distorted your view of yourself and your self-worth. God's freedom can redefine you and make you whole. Choose today to reflect the Spirit of God and His glory. Make this day the day when you stop giving life to negative thoughts of yourself and others.

Assignment: When a negative thought comes into your mind, replace it with a positive one. Look for the positive things in the day. Imagine that others can hear what you're thinking. If you don't want them to hear it, stop thinking it. Mirror the glory of God through your thought life; then everyone will be able to see how truly beautiful you really are.

Prayer Guide

Dad, I need You really bad today. I have spent a lifetime fighting the negative thoughts and words I say to myself and which others have said to me. They really hurt and have caused me to doubt You and the abilities You have given me. Please forgive me for my negative thoughts, and I forgive those who have said or thought negative things about me. I ask that You would help me today to reflect Your glory and Spirit to myself, and to others. I want my life to be easy to read. Lord, I am Your epistle and I want to mirror Your glory through my life. I will walk in Your ways, Lord. I accept the freedom I gain from following Your Word. I love You, Lord, as well as myself and others. I am stepping into the beauty of holiness, and it will become an entire way of life for me. Receive this prayer, I humbly ask, and help me to grow in Your daily love. In Jesus' name, Amen!

Action Step

DAY THREE

Calming My Spirit

SCRIPTURE READING: PHILIPPIANS 4:6–9

MEMORY VERSE
Be careful for nothing; but in every thing by prayer and
supplication with thanksgiving let your requests be made
known unto God.
(Philippians 4:6)

The hustle and bustle of rushing around is our way of life today. Many of our daily schedules are so jam-packed with things we're doing or planning to do that our minds don't have any quiet time to reflect. How can our minds be quiet in a racing world? First, we will have to examine and access what is truly important. Second, we must prioritize our lives by using the Word of God, which tells us to seek Him first in everything, no matter what the situation:

> *But seek ye first the kingdom of God, and his*
> *righteousness; and all these things*
> *shall be added unto you.*
> (Matthew 6:33)

This is how you will receive divine instructions and opportunities that create a view of thankfulness. Believe me, sometimes it can be really hard to seek out the good in your life in tough circumstances. To see the blessing in your life, you may even need to ask God to show you how He sees your situation.

The scripture reading today teaches us how to train our minds. We will need to learn and practice thinking on things that are true, honest, just, and pure. In today's racy world, we need to focus on things that generate the peace of God in our lives. God's Word gives us a really easy formula for calming our spirit. We should learn His Word and receive His Word, which means to accept it without question. Then we need to do His Word for the peace of God to be with us.

Your spirit will calm when you have good communication with the Lord. Seek Him, pray in every circumstance, slow down sometimes, and reduce the number of commitments you have in a day. Take time every day to pray and study the Word. If you practice one biblical principle per day, you will experience the peace of God, which will calm your spirit.

In rough times, reduce your stress by reducing commitments. Get regular exercise, eat healthy, drink plenty of water, and get plenty of rest. This will enable you to make better choices through tough times and not pig out on sweets and junk food. And, by the way, tough times don't last forever!

Prayer Guide

Lord, I need Your help to calm my spirit today. I invite You to lead me and guide my every decision. I need You so much, Jesus, so please help me to live for You every minute of the day. I have been working on a closer relationship with You and I need You to continue helping me to control what I think and how I see my situations. Sometimes things can be really hard, but you have promised me Your peace. So I'm asking You for your peace in my mind, body, soul, and spirit. Wherever I need Your healing in my emotions, please give me it this day. In Jesus' name, Amen!

Action Step

DAY FOUR

The Anxiety Cure

MEMORY VERSE

Put on therefore, as the elect of God, holy and beloved,
bowels of mercies, kindness, humbleness of mind,
meekness, longsuffering.
(Colossians 3:12)

The cure for anxiety is all in the dress. How are you dressing yourself these days? Christian beauty has a look, and even a smell. The fashion style of a woman of God should radiate the presence and peace of God.

Here is a simple test to determine what fashion statements you are making. First, if you suffer from anxiety, you might be wearing worry, frustration, anger, or depression. Make sure that you seek medical help to rule out any undiagnosed health condition or disease. Hormonal or chemical imbalances in your body can contribute to mood disorders.

Next, examine your spiritual and emotional state. Does it line up with the Word of God? Here is another simple test: examine yourself by today's memory verse. Colossians 3:12 states that we must put on our Christian virtue. Choose your daily wardrobe. Dressing for success begins with putting on the "bowels of mercies" (this just means compassion).

Then add kindness, humbleness of mind, meekness, and long-suffering. And no holiness closet should ever be without forbearing and forgiving one another in love and charity. These are the perfect outfits one should wear. If you dress in this way, you will have no room for worry, anxiety, or depression.

Let's clean out your spiritual closet by tossing the old garments out and shop for new ones in the Word of God. Practice makes perfect in the Word. While you are learning how to dress, God's peace will be upon you and His grace will flow out of your heart. To obtain good success, Scripture states:

> *This book of the law shall not depart out of thy mouth;*
> *but thou shalt meditate therein day and night, that*
> *thou mayest observe to do according to all that is written*
> *therein: for then thou shalt make thy way prosperous,*
> *and then thou shalt have good success.*
> (Joshua 1:8)

Prayer Guide

O Father, I have been wearing these old clothes for way too long. They have caused me to identify with the world's belief system, which produces stress, anxiety, anger, and depression. Please forgive me of my sinful behavior and renew in me a right spirit. In Your Word, you said that You purchased our healing through Your shed blood, and that by Your strips we are healed. So please heal me of any spirit of worry, anxiety, fear, anger, or depression (Isaiah 53:5). And if I need to see a physician for any underlying health condition, please guide the Physician and reveal the cause and proper treatment. Replace negative behaviors with positive ones, and fill me up with Your peace, joy, and grace. I forgive those who have hurt or offended me, and forgive me if I have hurt or offended anyone. I need Your wisdom and guidance in order to dress myself for spiritual success. I truly desire the spiritual maturity that comes from walking in Your beauty of holiness. Shine out of me daily and keep me, dear Lord, this day. I love You so much, and let Your Word of peace and rest abide in my life forever. In closing this prayer, I give You back Your Word: *"The grace of the Lord Jesus Christ, and the love of God, and the communion of the Holy Ghost, be with you all. Amen"* (2 Corinthians 13:14).

Action Step

DAY FIVE

The Alabaster Box

SCRIPTURE READING: JOHN 12:1–8

MEMORY VERSE

That he might sanctify and cleanse it with the washing of water by the word, that he might present it to himself a glorious church, not having spot, or wrinkle, or any such thing; but that it should be holy and without blemish.
(Ephesians 5:26–27)

The story of the alabaster box is about a woman named Mary Magdalene.

Who was Mary? She was a woman who encountered the transforming power of our Lord Jesus Christ through her act of surrender. Mary was a prostitute, a woman out of whom Jesus cast seven demons. She was also the sister of both Martha and Lazarus.[4] Martha was the one who told Jesus, *"If thou hadst been here, my brother had not died"* (John 11:21). But one day her story changed and she became a woman who broke her alabaster box and poured her costly oil on our Savior and wiped His feet

---

[4] Elizabeth Fletcher, *Women in the Bible*, "Mary Magdalene's Story." Date of access: September 29, 2015 (http://www.womeninthebible.net/women-bible-old-new-testaments/mary-magdalene).

with her hair. Now, who is this Mary? She is the one who loved Jesus enough to break her alabaster box and pour her precious oil as an act of intense love and devotion.

Understanding this moment in history, you need to understand the importance of alabaster. Most believe that the box was wooden, but it was not, because the oil would have leaked out. Alabaster is actually a type of marble, from the rock family. This type of stone is made from a mixture of fine-grained calcium sulphate. Its normal color is translucent white, but as the water in this compound evaporates, the alabaster darkens and develops brown veins.[5] In that period, women saved these alabaster boxes for when they got married.[6] Basically, it was her trust, or her wealth.

What is yours? Examine the characteristic of your life to see if you are made of wood. If so, you will be a leaky vessel. If you're an aged alabaster vessel with water evaporation, you need to return to the Lord for a refresher. And finally, if you are pure alabaster, then break it and pour your oil upon the Lord. Stay watered through a personal relationship with Christ, because alabaster is not as pretty when it loses its water.

Now, let's put the pieces of this story together. Mary, a sinner, came to Jesus broken. Once she received Christ, she was willing to break her most valuable treasure to demonstrate her love for Him. Can you do this? Are you willing to break your own alabaster box—yours maybe, your hopes and dreams, your success, your career, even your husband? What are you willing to break for Jesus? God needs us to come to Him fully broken so that He can make something new out of our broken pieces. He loves shattered dreams, and He gets excited over impossible situations.

---

[5] Ronnie Rosenbach, *Basic Source Catalog*, "Alabaster: A Primer." (Rohnert Park, CA: The Basic Source, 2003), 7–8.

[6] Kevin Knight, ed., *New Advent*, "Alabaster." Date of access: September 29, 2015 (http://www.newadvent.org/cathen/01244b.htm). Quoting: Florentine Bechtel, "Alabaster," *The Catholic Encyclopedia, Volume One* (New York, NY: Robert Appleton Company, 1907).

So are you willing to break your alabaster box and pour your costly oil upon our Savior? Are you willing to surrender everything? Mary did, and as a result the Lord said that Mary would be remembered through history for her act of love.

Jesus, our loving Savior, is the answer to your every care and concern. Jesus will change the direction of your life. Wash yourself in His shed blood and you will be cleansed. Water yourself in His Word daily and you will grow in His ways. Finally, refresh yourself, by allowing God to flow through you. This will keep you spiritually healthy in the Lord. Wash, water, and flow, and then you will grow. Are you willing to be broken for the Lord?

Prayer Guide

Yes, Lord, I am willing to be broken for You! Oh gracious Father, I realize that in order for You to use me and get the most glory out of my life, I must submit my broken pieces to You. Lord, I am broken and I need You so much. Please, Lord, I surrender my life to You. Please forgive me of all my sins. I want nothing to come between us anymore. Lord, loving You will now become the most important treasure in my life. You have my alabaster box and all my oil. Through brokenness, I am made whole. Today I will praise and worship You as I walk in the beauty of holiness; use my life as it pleases You, Lord. In Jesus' name, Your broken daughter. Amen!

Action Step

DAY SIX

Reflection and Assignment

1. Scriptures Review:
Name one truth you have gained from each day.
- 1 Chronicles 16:10–12
- 2 Corinthians 3:1–18
- Philippians 4:6–9
- Colossians 3:12–17
- John 12:1–8

2. Summarize one key truth from each devotionals lesson.
-
-
-
-
-

3. What is the most important behavioral change you will make regarding your mental and emotional health?

4. List one key prayer truth you have given to the Lord each day.

-
-
-
-
-

5. To whom or for what do you need to seek the Lord's forgiveness?

-
-
-
-
-

DAY SEVEN

Your Corporate Day of Worship

MEMORY VERSE

Not forsaking the assembling of ourselves together, as the manner of some is; but exhorting one another: and so much the more, as ye see the day approaching
(Hebrews 10:25)

Prayer Guide

Father in obedience and submission to your authority we honor You this day by being present in active corporate worship with others in Jesus name. Amen!

Week Two

BEAUTY CARE: MATTERS OF THE HEART

And above all things have fervent charity among yourselves:
for charity shall cover the multitude of sins.
(1 Peter 4:8)

DAY EIGHT

The Heart Condition

SCRIPTURE READING: I JOHN 4:4–12

MEMORY VERSE
Jesus said unto him, Thou shalt love the Lord thy God
with all thy heart, and with all thy soul,
and with all thy mind.
(Matthew 22:37)

O ur love comes from the heart. So let's examine our hearts and how they function.

Naturally, the human heart has four chambers (the left and right atrium, and the left and right ventricle). The flow of life comes from the beating and pumping of blood. Blood flow is the key to human life. The rhythm and timing of the heartbeat determines how blood flows through the body.

Spiritually, one's heart should have a flow. The word states, *"Keep thy heart with all diligence; for out of it are the issues of life"* (Proverbs 4:23). The spiritual heart identifies our state and relationship with God. How we are defined as believers is based on what comes out of our hearts. If we are full of God's love, Word, and holiness, then that is what will come out of us.

But if our hearts are full of hurt, pain, unforgiveness, or bitterness, then these issues will come out in our character.

The reason the Word tells us to be diligent at keeping our hearts is because it's hard work to keep a clean heart when one experiences heartbreak and pain. Well, the Lord knew this about us, because He made us. So He gave us the medicine, through His Word, to solve our heart conditions.

First, recognize that we are human and we make mistakes. God knows this and He loves us anyway. We must recognize that the love of God can only flow through us if it's in us. The love of God can only be shown through the heart of a person who has obtained the love of God. We are the demonstrators of God's love. His love is perfect; it does not judge or become offended, and most of all it does not hold onto unforgiveness or grudges.

Accept God's love for you through forgiveness. Forgive yourself and others who may have caused some of your heartache. You can love your way out of any heart condition. Love in action can cover a multitude of sin.

And above all things have fervent charity among
yourselves: for charity shall cover the multitude of sins.
(1 Peter 4:8)

Prayer Guide

Dear Lord, You are the greatest demonstrator of what real love looks like. Enable us to love others the way Your Word tells us to. I ask You to heal my heart condition and create in me a clean heart. As Psalm

51:10 says, *"Create in me a clean heart, O God; and renew a right spirit within me."* May I serve You and others better. Today help me start fresh with a clean heart, mind, and soul/spirit, so the love of God may flow through my life freely. Amen!

Action Step

DAY NINE

What's Love Got to Do with It?

SCRIPTURE READING: 1 CORINTHIANS 13:1–13

MEMORY VERSE

*Behold, I stand at the door, and knock: if any man hear
my voice, and open the door, I will come in to him, and
will sup with him, and he with me.*
(Revelation 3:20)

I n 1984, Tina Turner asked the world a famous question: "What's love got to do with it?" Well, in 2013 she gave the answer: "Everything!" When she married her companion of twenty-seven years, Turner said, "It's that happiness that people talk about, when you wish for nothing, when you can finally take a deep breath and say, 'Everything is good.'… It's a wonderful place to be."[7] After her abusive first marriage,

---

[7] Lesley Messer, *ABC News*, "Tina Turner Calls Married Life 'A Wonderful Place to Be.'" January 26, 2013 (http://abcnews.go.com/blogs/entertainment/2013/07/tina-turner-calls-married-life-a-wonderful-place-to-be/).

she wasn't quick to jump into a marriage commitment again. That's understandable considering her life story. But in spite of her difficult past, at the age of seventy-three years old, Tina launched a new story; she married the man who had waited twenty-seven years for her. Now that is love!

So what's your love story? Love has everything to do with Jesus's love story for each one of us. How long have you kept Jesus waiting for you? His Word says that He knocks on your door:

> *Behold, I stand at the door, and knock: if any man hear*
> *my voice, and open the door, I will come in to him, and*
> *will sup with him, and he with me.*
> (Revelation 3:20)

There are so many secular songs about love. "Love is a secondhand emotion" and "It takes a fool to learn that love don't love nobody" are lines from old love songs. These are wrong, though. Love should be our first emotion. If we truly loved one another the way God wanted us to, this world would be different. God would be pleased if we could demonstrate it to the world. Our love can bring peace to the earth. A situation can be changed through our love. Our love can restore, heal, and even deliver a soul. Love has absolutely everything to do with our lives.

As John 3:16 says, *"For God so loved the world, that he gave his only begotten Son…"* He gave us the most precious part of Himself. How awesome is that? What will your love give today? Forgiveness is love. Compassion and understanding is love. Freedom from depression and despair can be overcome through love. Let us practice loving ourselves, no matter how many mistakes we have made. Forgive yourself. Love others by allowing God's love to flow through you.

We are known to the world by the love we show them. The true meaning of love has been demonstrated. Love is giving, patient, and kind. The love of Christ is the way to step into the beauty of holiness.

Assignment: Today you will need to start practicing how to love. Demonstrate love this week through random acts of kindness. It can be as simple as a smile or an encouraging word. Or you could take someone to lunch or pay for a stranger's groceries or gas for their car. Get creative and have fun with love.

Prayer Guide

Lord, I need Your love in order to love. I have been hurt so many times when love was not returned. I have sometimes used love as a weapon and a form of manipulation to get what I wanted. You have never done that to me, but I have done that to You and others. I repent and seek Your forgiveness. I will not allow my love to come from a place of injury. My heart needs your healing love now. Have mercy on me, wash me clean, and equip me to love again. Create in me a clean heart and renew in me a right spirit, so that I will be able to love the way You intended me to. As Psalms 51:8 says, *"Make me to hear joy and gladness"* again. Receive this prayer, I humbly ask, in Your precious name of love, Jesus. Amen!

Action Step

DAY TEN

The Recipe for Grace

SCRIPTURE READING: ROMANS 12:1–10

MEMORY VERSE
*And be ye kind one to another, tenderhearted, forgiving
one another, even as God for Christ's sake hath forgiven
you.*
(Ephesians 4:32)

If I could scream from a roof top, I would say, "Be kind to one another!" Be a sincerely gracious and kindhearted person to each other without any hidden agendas or selfish motives. The word of God actually tells us to be "tenderhearted" (Ephesians 4:32).

Now, how can one who lives for God do this in a world where success is basically motivated through self-seeking? God's Word gives us a recipe for His grace. The term recipe is defined as "a set of instructions and/or formula for making something from various ingredients."[8] God has a formula for a grace-filled life. Grace is considered unmerited favor. That just means that God gives us things we don't deserve. Knowing that about God can help us

---

[8] *Merriam-Webster*, "Recipe." Date of access: April 21, 2017 (https://www.merriam-webster.com/dictionary/recipe).

to love God more and be grateful for the opportunities that come into our lives. A life that pleases God will carry a measure of grace.

Throughout the following scriptures, the term "measure" is used. Measure is defined as "an adequate or due portion."[9] Our measure of grace is a direct gift or blessing from God. Our obedience to the Word of God determines the amount of grace He gives to each of us. You are unique, and within that uniqueness God will dispense grace unto you based on your purpose in life. Your actions, dedication, and faith will determine the fullness of the grace supplied to you.

Based on the Word of God, here are five scriptures that should become a part of your daily recipe for a grace-filled life:

A BALANCED LIFE:
But thou shalt have a perfect and just weight, a perfect and just measure shalt thou have: that thy days may be lengthened in the land which the Lord thy God giveth thee.
(Deuteronomy 25:15)

PURPOSE OR MEANING IN LIFE:
Lord, make me to know mine end, and the measure of my days, what it is: that I may know how frail I am.
(Psalm 39:4)

A NONJUDGMENTAL LIFE
For with what judgment ye judge, ye shall be judged: and with what measure ye mete, it shall be measured to you again.
(Matthew 7:2)

---

[9] *Merriam-Webster*, "Measure." Date of access: April 21, 2017 (https://www.merriam-webster.com/dictionary/measure).

A Hearer and Doer of the Word of God Life:

*And he said unto them, Take heed what ye hear: with
what measure ye mete, it shall be measured to you: and
unto you that hear shall more be given.*
(Mark 4:24)

A Fellowship in Unity Life

*From whom the whole body fitly joined together and
compacted by that which every joint supplieth, according
to the effectual working in the measure of every part,
maketh increase of the body unto
the edifying of itself in love.*
(Ephesians 4:16)

Mix these five areas of Scripture with daily prayer, praise, and worship
and you will become a trophy of His grace.

*And God is able to make all grace abound toward you;
that ye, always having all sufficiency in all things, may
abound to every good work...*
(2 Corinthians 9:8)

Prayer Guide

Lord, I pray Your Word, which has been supplied to
me today through this devotion. You are the dispenser
of grace in my life. Your Word says, *"But unto every one
of us is given grace according to the measure of the gift of*

Christ" (Ephesians 4:7). Please, dear Lord, help me to become a trophy of Your grace for Your glory. I love and appreciate Your goodness in my life. Forgive me of anything I have done, thought, or felt that doesn't please You, because I want to please You in all areas of my life. Help me to organize my daily schedule, and to reduce drama and stress in my life, so I can have a God-centered life that strives for excellence. Please receive this prayer, I humbly ask, in the precious name of Jesus. Amen!

Action Step

DAY ELEVEN

A Satisfied Soul

SCRIPTURE READING: DANIEL 10:8–12

MEMORY VERSE

*Thou wilt shew me the path of life: in thy presence is
fulness of joy; at thy right hand there are pleasures for
evermore.*
(Psalm 16:11)

During a recovery season in my life many years ago, I attended
and served for three years in the Celebrate Recovery ministry at
Celebration Church in Columbia, Maryland. As a servant leader, never
did I think that I would obtain a lasting and sustaining emotional healing
that would unlock and heal years of deep hidden pain within me. But
it did! In order to serve as a leader in the ministry, we each had to go
through the program ourselves. After all, leaders sometimes need healing,
too. It took me one year to graduate (see Appendix A).

The opening prayer, used in the Celebrate Recovery program
meetings, is called the Serenity Prayer:

God grant me the serenity to accept the things I cannot
change,
the courage to change the things I can,
and the wisdom to know the difference.
Living one day at a time, enjoying one moment at a time;
accepting hardship as a pathway to peace;
taking, as Jesus did,
this sinful world as it is,
not as I would have it;
trusting that You will make all things right
if I surrender to Your will;
so that I may be reasonably happy in this life
and supremely happy with You forever in the next.
Amen.[10]

For the longest time, this prayer annoyed me so much. There were
times when I didn't even want to say it in the weekly recovery meetings.
One day, about six months into my personal recovery journey, I was asked
to open up the service with the prayer. I recited it from memory and my
spirit just broke. I finally asked the Lord to help me to change the things
that I could, and to give me the wisdom to know and recognize the things
that were not in my control. That evening, all of the things that had ever
happened to me over which I had no control seemed to flood my mind. I
had carried so many secret issues, hurts, and hang-ups buried deep inside
me. They affected many areas of my life. I was often guarded, insecure, and
my lack of self-worth and value plagued me despite my accomplishments
and successes. Inside me, I always felt that I was never good enough, even
though I had put in a lot of hard work and determination to reach my
goals. Well, through the program, I had to learn how to rescue my trapped

[10] John Baker, *Stepping Out of Denial into God's Grace: Participant's Guide One* (Grand
Rapids, MI: Zondervan, 2012), 14. Quoting the Prayer for Serenity, by Reinhold Niebuhr.

self, release the past, and realize that I was good enough for God's love just the way I was. When I did, I became a recovered, satisfied soul!

To become a satisfied soul, we need to seek the Lord for His universal cure—his serenity, which is "the state or quality of being serene [calm or tranquil]."[11] If a person is satisfied, that can mean they are content or confidently pleased with their life. Whether someone is single, married, divorced, or widowed, it's essential to foster contentment and a heart that wants to please God.

The Bible talks about a universal cure called "The Balm of Gilead." This was a rare and precious medicinal perfume which was given to people to extend healing and health.[12]

> *Is there no balm in Gilead; is there no physician there?*
> *Why then is not the health of the daughter*
> *of my people recovered?*
> (Jeremiah 8:22)

Will you become the satisfied daughter who has a life that's been graced with our Savior's balm?

What is the soul? It is "the principle of life, feeling, thought, and action in humans, regarded as a distinct entity separate from the body, and commonly held to be separable inexistence from the body; the spiritual part of humans as distinct from the physical part."[13] Your soul is where God wants to live permanently. He wants to abide in you, with you, and around you. He wants you to receive the greatest deliverance ever, to become satisfied with Him and in Him alone. Receive His healing balm today and you will become a satisfied soul.

---

[11] *Merriam-Webster*, "Serenity." Date of access: April 21, 2017 (https://www.merriam-webster.com/dictionary/serenity).

[12] *Wikipedia*, "Balm of Gilead." Date of access: April 21, 2017 (https://en.wikipedia.org/wiki/Balm_of_Gilead).

[13] *Dictionary.com*, "Soul." Date of access: April 21, 2017 (http://www.dictionary.com/browse/soul).

Prayer Guide

Lord, all You want is for me to use Your word in my life. As Proverbs 4:22 says, *"For they are life unto those that find them, and health to all their flesh."* I desire your joy in my life, through applying your balm of Gilead. I surrender my life to You today, and I give You complete control over my heart, emotions, and will. Father, all You have ever wanted me to do is seek You first, and Your kingdom, freedom, liberty, and peace. Please, Lord, will You fill me up, so that I can be a vessel that can dispense Your love, healing balm, and peace to others? I declare and decree this day to become a satisfied soul, in Jesus' precious name, Amen!

Action Step

Managed Care

SCRIPTURE READING: MARK 12:29–33

MEMORY VERSE
Look not every man on his own things,
but every man also on the things of others.
(Philippians 2:4)

O ne day while I was taking a morning walk through the neighborhood, I happened to notice a bird standing near the sidewalk instead of being near the pond. I noticed it on my very first lap. I thought it was so neat that it wasn't scared of me. I even took a picture of it and how beautiful the scene was. I passed three more times and thought to myself, *Wow, it's still standing there.* Then I looked around and I saw that this bird had some friends sitting on both sides of the pond, not moving but watching. I walked past the fourth time, and thought, *It's strange for this bird to still be in the same spot. I wonder why it hasn't moved.*

I had been walking for almost an hour and the bird still hadn't moved.

On my final lap, the bird flapped its wings as I passed it. Then I stopped and noticed that the bird was standing on one leg. Yes, the bird was injured. That was why it had been standing there with its friends watching out for it. They weren't playing or swimming, which was the norm. They were just sitting on the side of the pond, looking at their injured friend. Well, needless to say, I went into rescue mode. I felt so bad that I had walked for over an hour before even noticing that the bird was injured. I called animal rescue.

"Please try to save the bird," I said. "Call me back and let me know if the bird can be saved."

Well, I ask you today, are you overly consumed with yourself, cell phone, or social media? Our busy lifestyles have caused us to not notice the injured souls all around us. Sometimes we just don't notice opportunities to serve others. That day, I felt the Lord's conviction that it took me way too long to notice that there was something wrong.

What about you? Are you so busy that you don't notice the needs of others? The title of this devotional is "Managed Care." Are you caring about others, serving, helping, being a friend in need, or are you just too busy? Today's scriptures talk about us being good neighbors. It's the second commandment after loving God with all your heart: *"Thou shalt love thy neighbour as thyself"* (Mark 12:31).

To improve your heart condition, start managing your area of care. Create a care day each month. Schedule caring for someone in some small way as a monthly event. It will soften your heart and cause you to experience God's love in your life more. Care about others, your family, your friends, your church, your community, your neighbors, your coworkers, and even the strangers you meet. Opportunities to care are all around us, so manage your care!

Prayer Guide

Lord, You call us friend. You demonstrate daily how much You love and care for me. In this world, I can get so busy with my own life that I forget to be loving and caring to others more or less fortunate than me. As one of my steps toward the beauty of holiness today, I will begin to set aside time to manage caring and serving others more often. Help me, dear Lord, to daily see the opportunities that are all around my circle of influence. Through my caring effort, may a soul be loved and won for Your Kingdom. Amen!

Action Step

DAY THIRTEEN

Reflection and Assignment

1. Scriptures Review:

Name one truth you have gained from each day.

- 1 John 4:4–12
- 1 Corinthians 13:1–13
- Romans 12:1–10
- Daniel 10:8–12
- Mark 12:29–33

2. Summarize one key truth from each devotionals lesson.

-
-
-
-
-

3. What is the most important behavioral change you will make regarding your mental and emotional health?

4. List one key prayer truth you have given to the Lord each day.

-
-
-
-
-

5. To whom or for what do you need to seek the Lord's forgiveness?

-
-
-
-
-

DAY FOURTEEN

Your Corporate Day of Worship

MEMORY VERSE

*Praise ye the Lord. I will praise the Lord
with my whole heart, in the assembly of the upright,
and in the congregation.*
(Psalm 111:1)

Prayer Guide

O Lord, you are the lifter up of my head. I give you my whole heart in worship today. Use me Lord as an instrument for Your glory in praise and worship. I actively seek You in a spirit of humility and thanksgiving, in Jesus name. Amen!

Week Three

BEAUTY CARE: HOLINESS IS SKIN DEEP

But the Lord said unto Samuel, Look not on his countenance,
or on the height of his stature; because I have refused
him: for the Lord seeth not as man seeth; for man
looketh on the outward appearance, but the
Lord looketh on the heart.

(1 Samuel 16:7)

DAY FIFTEEN

The Call for Developing an Excellent Spirit

SCRIPTURE READING: DANIEL 1:1–20

MEMORY VERSE
*But to the saints that are in the earth, and to the
excellent, in whom is all my delight.*
(Psalms 16:3)

There is a price for living a fruitful life of excellence in the Lord. It is called discipline! The Bible used Daniel to give us insight into the qualities of what an "excellent spirit" should look like: stability in the faith, consistency in character during difficult times, confidence and assurance in God, skill in learning, wisdom and understanding of the Word of God, and workers who lead to God-given favor in leadership positions. The secular world's term for this is "perfectionism," a learned behavior that is not healthy for a person's spirit. It can directly trigger anxiety and depressive disorders.

Because perfectionism can be hidden within striving for success or overachievement, we tend not to recognize that one's efforts can be motivated by insecurity or the fear of failure. Since we live in a world that's based on a competitive reward system, we tend to be socialized to believe that our accomplishments are directly associated with our own value and self-worth.[14]

The difference between an excellent spirit and perfectionism are:

An excellent spirit	A spirit of perfectionism
The purpose of your heart is to please the Lord.	Your best efforts are never good enough.
You are a prayerful and obedient servant.	Your self-worth is associated with performance.
You are a faithful, steadfast, and consistent believer.	Your are never satisfied with the work you have completed.
You have a daily devotional prayer life.	The primary root of your procrastination is a fear of failure.

Through behavioral modification and the Word of God, you can learn to develop an excellent spirit. The Lord identified some important aspects of this in the book of Daniel. First and most important, Daniel 1:8 states that Daniel *"purposed in his heart that he would not defile himself…"*

---

[14] Mary M. Christopher and Jennifer Shewmaker, "The Relationship of Perfectionism to Affective Variables in Gifted and Highly Able Children." *Gifted Child Today*, Summer 2010, 20–30.

Second, Daniel and his friends lived clean and pure lives. They were also of royal blood, meaning that he had quality friends with good character. Finally, Daniel's strength came from having a daily prayer life that was consistently full of praise and thanksgiving. Daniel was faithful and those around him could find no fault or error in his life (Daniel 6:4).

Working toward developing an excellent spirit is a personal lifestyle choice, and it takes your salvation to a higher level which inspires you to want to be the best possible servant of the Lord. For me, it's a continual process of learning, applying, and committing my will to the Lord on a daily basis. As believers, we must live Spirit-led lives in which we do what God wants us to do and be who God wants us to be!

Please don't get me wrong: we should all be our true and authentic selves, which means discovering who God has made us to be. We are all unique, special, and have been given a lifelong task to fulfill on this earth. Are you ready to start working on developing the excellent spirit within you?

Assignment: Examine your relationships and close friendships. What have you discovered about them? Does something need to change?

Prayer Guide

Dearest Father, thank You for all You have been and done for me. Please forgive me if I have led a life of perfectionism and didn't know it. I now realize that it doesn't please You, and I want so much to please You. It is really important, Lord, that I purpose in my heart not to willfully sin against You, others, or myself. Help me to live a life of excellence, as Psalms 16:3 directs me. I want to start developing qualities that please You.

So, Father, lead and guide me to be one who trusts in You and is grateful and satisfied with Your goodness and provisions. Lord, help me to seek Your wisdom, counsel, and guidance for making life decisions. I praise You for my salvation, fellowship, and growing consistency in devoting a portion of each day to You in my devotional and prayer life. I humbly ask that You accept this prayer as I work on the inner part of me, stepping into the beauty of holiness through this devotional series. Amen!

Action Step

DAY SIXTEEN

Lord, You Want Me to Do What?

SCRIPTURE REFERENCE: COLOSSIANS 3:1–7

MEMORY VERSE

For I know the thoughts that I think toward you, saith the Lord, thoughts of peace, and not of evil, to give you an expected end.
(Jeremiah 29:11)

Have you ever noticed how a simple prayer request can turn your life around?

As you were speaking the words, perhaps your heart was not as attentive as in times past; or perhaps you were so focused on the need that you prayed earnestly with little thought to how God would answer. Did you know that a simple prayer request can turn your life upside-down, or for some right-side-up? Welcome to God's answer to your prayer request. You have just opened the door to the Lord's transition process.

Transition means "passage from one state, stage, subject, or place to another."[15] Another source describes transitions as either a positive or negative movement, shift, or change that can take place throughout one's life.[16] Many of us want change in our lives, but we aren't really ready to pay the price. Answered prayers cost something. So taking this journey toward radiating the beauty of holiness will cost you something.

Transition causes a type of death to the self, or a putting off of the old ways of the flesh (Colossians 3:1–7). You may ask, what has happened to my life? It may feel like a bomb exploded and life seems really crazy for a while. Are you willing to trust God for times such as these? Are you willing? Will you trust God's process to work in your life? I promise you, He is not going to kill you. He gets no glory in that. But what He does want is for you to allow your flesh to die, so that He can get all of the glory out of your life. He has a plan for your life (Jeremiah 29:11). While you were praying a simple prayer, you may have touched on something deeply rooted in the heart of God. Trust God and hope for the future.

The Bible contains many examples of people being made useful through dealing with God in their lives. Some endured transitional trials and went on to fulfill their God-given purpose. The life they once knew was gone.

- Can you walk away from the familiar? This may cost you some relationships, friendships, and even some family.
- How about a change in location? Are you willing to move? Will you change your employment, your career paths, and your lifestyle, whether scaling up or down?

---

[15] *Merriam-Webster*, "Transition." Date of access: April 21, 2017 (https://www.merriam-webster.com/dictionary/transition).

[16] *The Mind Unleashed*, "10 Ways to Transition from a Negative to a Positive Thinker." January 21, 2015 (http://themindunleashed.com/2015/01/10-ways-transition-negative-positive-thinker.html).

- On the emotional side, it could cause a period of loneliness, quiet, reflection, and maybe even a few tears, because you won't be able to explain what is happening to you yet.

This can be hard on people who know and love you. Before, you always told them everything, but now you can tell them nothing, because God isn't telling you. You have to simply trust God. Transition can make you feel nervous, fearful, afraid, and unique. It will cause you to second-guess yourself and everything you are doing. Take heart, for you will not stay in that place long; it is just the in-between process to realize a very great and precious promise (2 Peter 1:4).

> *Wherefore seeing we also are compassed about with so*
> *great a cloud of witnesses, let us lay aside every weight,*
> *and the sin which doth so easily beset us, and let us run*
> *with patience the race that is set before us...*
> (Hebrews 12:1)

You are in great company with the many who have endured and passed their transition test.

Important: Seek forgiveness for any sins, offenses, and roots of bitterness. These get in the way of so many things in our lives. These can be tricky, because sometimes we like them and they hide under some pleasures. Watch and pray!

Prayer Guide

Dear Lord, please forgive me for sinful fear and my failure to trust You in the midst of a life transition.

Though I may not fully understand everything, I am fully persuaded that You have everything in control. I surrender to Your plans and purpose for my life. Please receive all the praise and glory from my life, in Jesus' name, Amen!

Action Step

DAY SEVENTEEN

The Reap Principle

SCRIPTURE READING: GENESIS 12:1–8

MEMORY VERSE

This book of the law shall not depart out of thy mouth;
but thou shalt meditate therein day and night, that
thou mayest observe to do according to all that is written
therein: for then thou shalt make thy way prosperous,
and then thou shalt have good success.
(Joshua 1:8)

God told Abraham, our father of many nations, to move his family—in other words, to relocate. God even asked him to change his name from Abram to Abraham. How many of you need a name change? I did. He will show you the way.

> *Now the Lord had said unto Abram, Get thee out of thy*
> *country, and from thy kindred, and from thy father's*
> *house, unto a land that I will shew thee…*
> (Genesis 12:1).

Sometimes the only way God can bless you and answer your prayers is to take you away from people, places, or things that don't respect Him or you. I always say that the nouns in our lives are where our issues, problems, and drama come from. You have got to manage the nouns in your life in order to obtain the blessings of His favor.

> *And I will make of thee a great nation,*
> *and I will bless thee, and make thy name great;*
> *and thou shalt be a blessing...*
> (Genesis 12:2)

Coming through the transition process, we will become a blessing. Now, isn't that interesting? You started out with a simple prayer request, which changed your entire life to make you a blessing to others. I'm pretty sure your original prayer request didn't ask for the transition process directly, nor did you know that the Lord's answer, in terms of transition or repositioning yourself, wouldn't be about you, but more about making you a blessing for others.

STUDY THE WORD OF GOD

Here are a few tips and scriptures to help you get through the transition process:

1. Bless the Lord at all times, even in the uncomfortable tearful moments:

> *I will bless the Lord at all times: his praise shall*
> *continually be in my mouth.*
> (Psalm 34:1)

2. You have got to seriously seek God for all guidance decisions and directions. There may be people, places, or things that should not go with you into your new season.

3. Being in the wilderness is only a moment. Rejoice, and again I say rejoice! When you know you are in the wilderness, you know that the promised land will be at the end of the transition. You rejoice, for He rejoices over you. Then you rejoice over Him. Get it and repeat!

Rejoice in the Lord always: and again I say, Rejoice.
(Philippians 4:4)

And the Lord thy God will make thee plenteous in every work of thine hand, in the fruit of thy body, and in the fruit of thy cattle, and in the fruit of thy land, for good: for the Lord will again rejoice over thee for good, as he rejoiced over thy fathers…
(Deuteronomy 30:9)

Watch and pray, that ye enter not into temptation: the spirit indeed is willing, but the flesh is weak.
(Matthew 26:41)

4. Study, study, and study some more. Memorize and become a doer of the Word, not a hearer only.

But be ye doers of the word, and not hearers only, deceiving your own selves.
(James 1:22)

Study to shew thyself approved unto God,
a workman that needeth not to be ashamed,
rightly dividing the word of truth.
(2 Timothy 2:15)

5. Apply the REAP principle: read, eat, absorb, and pray (with fasting).

Now, move forward into God's destiny and purpose for your life. It will take a lot of hard work on your part. You have to be willing to pay the price and do the time to be free. Becoming a vessel blessed with God's beauty of holiness requires you to grow in grace and His knowledge. Go and grow, knowing:

This book of the law shall not depart out of thy mouth;
but thou shalt meditate therein day and night, that
thou mayest observe to do according to all that is written
therein: for then thou shalt make thy way prosperous,
and then thou shalt have good success. Have not I
commanded thee? Be strong and of a good courage; be
not afraid, neither be thou dismayed: for the Lord thy
God is with thee whithersoever thou goest.
(Joshua 1:8–9)

Prayer Guide

Lord, I truly love You. Your Word and Your ways are amazing. I need You so much in my life that I am willing to follow Your script, meaning Your scriptures, because You have said that they are life to me. I surrender to the REAP lifestyle of living. Please help me to accomplish this daily, so that I can be a light for others. I will prepare myself for serving others, becoming a better server in You, in Jesus' name, Amen!

Action Step

DAY EIGHTEEN

Pacing God's Race

SCRIPTURE READING: MATTHEW 26:36–45 AND MALACHI 3:10

MEMORY VERSE
*And he cometh unto the disciples, and findeth them
asleep, and saith unto Peter, What, could ye not watch
with me one hour? Watch and pray, that ye enter not into
temptation: the spirit indeed is willing, but the flesh is
weak.*
(Matthew 26:40–41)

In this busy world, we are surrounded by the hustle and bustle of being driven to want more and do more to get more. Society teaches us how to manage our time in order to be more productive and therefore become more prosperous. But as Christians, God has given us His pace to follow through His Word. Matthew 26:40–41 states, *"Could ye not watch with me one hour? Watch and pray…"* His pace is much slower and more organized than most of ours. If we organize our time following His guidance, we will become much more productive than if we tried to do it all on our own.

What if we tithed ten percent of our time to the Lord, as instructed by Malachi 3:10? Some may refer to this as sweat equity, a real estate term that refers to putting a price on your personal labor. Our time can actually be viewed as a financial principle. This means that out of twenty-four hours a day, we should commit at least 2.4 hours to the Lord. If you dedicate this time to the Lord, it will improve and organize the pace of the other ninety percent of your day. Many Christians have become so busy that their lives have begun to closely resemble the fast-paced stressful living of the world. Before you even recognize it, you start giving the Lord your leftovers.

I found this out the hard way. Actually, I'm writing this particular devotional during my own recovery process from a stress-related illness. God used this situation to show me that I had become too driven, that I was pushing too hard to keep up with the world's pace. His loving hands showed me the importance of "balance." I took the opportunity to watch and pray, and incorporate some of the Lord's time management principles. This included seeking the Lord first, giving the Lord the firstfruits of my life—if possible the firstfruits of each day.

Start your day with both prayer and devotional time. This will make the other ninety percent of the day better and more manageable. Next, watch for overload through too many commitments. Schedule daily quiet time. This will allow you time to hear from God, giving Him headship over your life, which will allow Him to lead you better. And finally, if you break up the 2.4 hours of your tithing time, notice that it is actually doable.

Here is an example of a daily time-tithing schedule:
- Thirty minutes for morning prayer and devotions.
- Fifteen minutes for midday prayer and meditation.
- Fifteen minutes to make a melody in your heart through praise and worship songs or scripture.
- Fifteen to twenty minutes of giving by serving others to be a blessing. A random act of kindness goes a long way to encourage others, and it's a lot of fun too. Sometimes it can be as simple as an encouraging telephone call to someone who is sick or elderly.

- Thirty minutes to study the Word of God.
- Fifteen minutes at bedtime for prayers of thanksgiving for all the Lord did in your day. If you need Him to calm you down, ask Him to give you His peace for a sweet sleep.
- Total: approximately two hours.

You may have a different order, but as you can see, the time passes very quickly. You will gain God's pace for tithing time. As children of God, our time is in His hands. By making an effort to put God first in your life, the payoff will be big.

If you are reading this devotional, then you are seeing what God can do with your time. For me, I get to share the beauty of holiness with you, my reader. In this third week of your thirty-day plan, I challenge you to examine your life, because discipleship requires discipline, structure, and stewardship of both our time and resources.

Take Malachi's tithing instructions to the next level by tithing your time. God will be pleased and you will grow tremendously. Can you give the Lord one hour? I hope your answer will be yes and you will start working on this behavior change until you reach at least the 2.4 hours per day goal.

Prayer Guide

Lord, I admit that I need help in this area of pacing and organizing my time better. I have been burning the candle at both ends and my life is on fire. Please forgive me for becoming so focused on obtaining that I am just as stressed and burned out as the world. Lord, help me to be a good example of time stewardship. If I also need to improve in the area of tithing my financial resources, please direct me in that area as well. Allow me to continue to grow in Your Word and Your ways as I continue this journey of stepping into the beauty of holiness. Amen!

Action Step

DAY NINETEEN

Casting Down My Net

SCRIPTURE READING: MATTHEW 13:47–50

MEMORY VERSE

Now when he had left speaking, he said unto Simon,
Launch out into the deep, and let down your nets for a
draught. And Simon answering said unto him, Master,
we have toiled all the night, and have taken nothing:
nevertheless at thy word I will let down the net.
(Luke 5:4–5)

Net-casting is an important spiritual principle that we all must master. Our quality of life in God is dependent on our knowledge and experience of being able to cast our nets. The word *casting* can mean "something cast in a mold,"[17] whereas *cast* can mean "to throw or move (something) in a forceful way."[18]

---

[17] *Merriam-Webster*, "Casting." Date of access: April 21, 2017 (https://www.merriam-webster.com/dictionary/casting).

[18] *Merriam-Webster*, "Cast." Date of access: April 21, 2017 (https://www.merriam-webster.com/dictionary/cast).

Now, why would God tell us in His Word to cast down our nets? If you don't cast your net down, it will be the net that entangles you. We all have nets that can be used either for good or bad. Your own net can mold you like a doctor casts a broken limb. The Word states, *"Let the wicked fall into their own nets, whilst that I withal escape"* (Psalm 141:10). If you don't follow God's instructions in this area of your spiritual walk, you will be trapped in a battle that seems almost impossible to break out of.

Examine yourself through prayer and the Word of God to see if you have any of the following characteristics of a wicket net: bitterness, resentment, unbelief, unforgiveness, regret, fear, and a sense of guilt. These are just to name a few, but if any of these are present, you can be sure that your own net is entangling you.

Our God is truly rich in mercy and He has great compassion toward us, so just follow His directions through the Word and you will be able to replace the wicked net with a net that possess the fruit of the spirit (Galatians 5:22–23). Your net should contain the following: love, joy, peace, long-suffering, gentleness, goodness, and faith. By casting your net into the sea, God promises to make you a fisher of men. This is another instance where we gain by giving away. This will truly help you to step into the beauty of holiness.

We often become entangled in our own nets. We fight and fight, wondering why life is so hard in the Lord. Well, it may be that your net is in the way. Today, stop fighting and start casting! It will be so much fun to see what the Lord will do with your net when you cast it into the sea. See you in the sea!

Prayer Guide

O Lord, I am crying out to You today! I recognize that my life shows signs of being entangled in my own net. Dear Lord, please forgive me for not using my net the way You instructed me. I am so tired of fighting, Lord. I thought that it was the enemy, but in actuality some of it has been my own net. You want me to cast my net into the sea, so it will not entrap me. Lord, today and forever, help me to let down my net so that I can become a fisher of men! In Jesus' precious name, Amen!

Action Step

DAY TWENTY

Reflection and Assignment

1. Scriptures Review:
Name one truth you have gained from each day.
- Daniel 1:1–20
- Colossians 3:1–7
- Genesis 12:1–8
- Matthew 13:47–50
- Isaiah 40:28–31

2. Summarize one key truth from each devotionals lesson.
-
-
-
-
-

3. What is the most important behavioral change you will make regarding your mental and emotional health?

4. List one key prayer truth you have given to the Lord each day.

-
-
-
-
-

5. To whom or for what do you need to seek the Lord's forgiveness?

-
-
-
-
-

DAY TWENTY-TWO

Your Corporate Day of Worship

MEMORY VERSE

*Jesus said unto him, Thou shalt love the Lord thy God
with all thy heart, and with all thy soul,
and with all thy mind.*
(Matthew 22:37)

Prayer Guide

Their is a song that states,"I'm coming back to a heart of worship, and it is all about You, Jesus." It's all about You, Jesus! Today, as I enter into corporate worship, prepare me to have clean hands and a pure heart so that You will be pleased with my worship in Jesus name, Amen!

Week Four

BEAUTY CARE:
LIVING A LIFE OF WHOLENESS

But they that wait upon the Lord shall renew
their strength; they shall mount up with wings
as eagles; they shall run, and not be weary;
and they shall walk, and not faint.
(Isaiah 40:31)

DAY TWENTY-THREE

The Ultimate Cleanse

SCRIPTURE READING: EXODUS 12:1–28

MEMORY VERSE

Purge out therefore the old leaven, that ye may be a new lump, as ye are unleavened. For even Christ our passover is sacrificed for us: therefore let us keep the feast, not with old leaven, neither with the leaven of malice and wickedness; but with the unleavened bread of sincerity and truth.
(1 Corinthians 5:7–8)

The concepts of spring-cleaning and detoxing the body are nothing new. The origin of cleansing came from the Bible. The Lord designed the ultimate cleansing for the children of Israel. It was called preparation for the Passover. For a Jewish person, preparing for Passover was, and still is, a specific time during the year when they prepared their bodies and homes. The scripture is very specific as to the steps that were to be taken for purification for Passover. Today, Jewish people do this yearly to remember the struggle of their deliverance.[19]

---

[19] *Hebrew4Christians.com*, "Preparing for Passover." Date of access: May 26, 2017 (http://www. hebrew4christians.com/Holidays/Spring_Holidays/Pesach/Preparations/preparations.html).

From a health and wellness prospective, let's examine the dietary consumption.

And they shall eat the flesh in that night, roast with fire,
and unleavened bread; and with bitter herbs
they shall eat it.
(Exodus 12:8)

First, the verse speaks of using a young lamb no more than one year old. This ensures that the lamb doesn't have a lot of fat. Next, the scripture states that there was to be unleavened bread and bitter herbs. Unleavened bread means no yeast in anything that would be consumed during the seven-day cleansing process (Exodus 12:15). And finally, the bitter herbs were commonly horseradish, romaine lettuce, and endive. These bitter herbs represent the bitterness of slavery.[20]

Christ is our ultimate Passover. He sacrificed Himself for us (1 Corinthians 5:7–8). We can be made new through the process of cleansing. Cleansing ourselves through washing our lives in the Word of God is the key to being purified. We need to regularly do spring-cleaning, and we need to regularly detox ourselves from the things that cause us to sin. Each one of the Passover preparations are steps we can use in our lives today, both naturally and spiritually. It is good to detox our natural bodies regularly.

At least once per quarter we should fast from leaven (meaning yeasts). Next, we should detox and flush out are bodies with herbs such as parsley and celery. These are blood purifiers and diuretics that can help to cleanse toxins from the body. For seven days, make a parsley tea with lemon. Drink it first thing in the morning and you will feel the benefits. The

---

[20] *Dummies.com*, "The Symbolic Goods at a Passover Seder." Date of access: February 26, 2017 (http://www.dummies.com/education/holidays/the-symbolic-foods-at-a-passover-seder/).

next tip is to eat less meats. Lamb is recommended in the Bible because it has less fat than other meats. Refrain from eating fried food for a season. These are simple steps to help you cleanse both your soul/spirit and body.

In this devotion, we have learned that Christ provided the ultimate cleanse. In His Word, He provides us as believers with instructions on how to purify ourselves both naturally and spiritually.

Diet Selections	Natural Benefits	Spiritual Benefits
Unleavened bread[1] (no yeast products)	Reduces the production of yeast and carbohydrate (sugar) reactions in the body	This is symbolic of the removal of sin from our lives.
Lamb[2] (young, one year old)	Lower in fat and high in iron	This is symbolic of Jesus Christ being the Lamb of God.
Bitter herbs[3] (horseradish, romaine lettuce, endives, parsley, and celery)	These specific herbs are considered blood purifiers. They cleanse our bodies of toxins by flushing out our kidneys and liver.	The blood of Jesus is the ultimate sacrifice. There is life in the Blood.

- Eat fewer yeasted foods, and eat more vegetables and lean meats.
- Spiritually, have a regular cleansing of your mind, heart, and emotions through seeking forgiveness and repenting of any unconfessed sin.
- Study, read, and memorize the Bible. Let the truth of Scripture renew your mind and cleanse your heart.
- Acknowledge that Christ is your ultimate cleanser through His shed blood and the sacrifice He has already made for you.
- Believe that He wants you to reach the promised land of freedom and liberty in the body of Christ.
- Forgive yourself and others on a regular basis, so that you will not have to carry the burden of sin. Christ is our ultimate cleanser, our Savior, and our Passover Lamb!

Prayer Guide

Dear Lord, my great and mighty Passover Lamb, I thank You and praise You for the sacrifice You made for me and my sin. I come to You for Your help to keep my life clean and my body healthy and well for You to use me to be a blessing to others. I love Your Word, and I love the truth You have given in the scriptures from both the Old and New Testaments. Your instructions are life to me. Help me to live a better life! I ask You to give me insight, wisdom, and a heart's desire to study your Word daily. Please receive this prayer and answer, I humbly ask, in Jesus' name, Amen!

Action Step

DAY TWENTY-FOUR

Season All!

SCRIPTURE READING: MATTHEW 5:1–12

MEMORY VERSE
*What? know ye not that your body is the temple of the
Holy Ghost which is in you, which ye have of God,
and ye are not your own?*
(1 Corinthians 6:19)

Physical beauty in the arena of holiness also requires us to become disciplined and committed to taking personal responsibility for our own care. In order to demonstrate that you care about your body, balance your health through scheduling time for proper rest, exercise, and eating right. These basic lifestyle skills and behaviors are the foundation for caring for the "temple of God," your body, which houses His Spirit.

How are you doing at taking care of yourself? Ponder this thought:

*Ye are the salt of the earth: but if the salt
have lost his savour, wherewith shall it be salted?
it is thenceforth good for nothing, but to be cast out,
and to be trodden under foot of men.*
(Matthew 5:13)

Are you salty enough to season others with your God-given spirit and beauty of holiness?

Naturally, the body needs a small amount of salt. Salt is considered an essential substance for sustaining life and preserving food, and it can keep things fresh and cause them to last longer.[21]

However, salt can also cause diseases in the body if it's eaten too much. According to the Institute of Medicine, the recommended daily allowance of salt for the average American is 2,300 milligrams per day (one teaspoon).[22] For African Americans and those sensitive to salt, the recommended daily allowance of salt is just 1,500 milligrams per day (three-quarters of a teaspoon). African-Americans are genetically at higher risk for high blood pressure, heart disease, and stroke.[23] [24]

Many times salt is hidden in our foods and we don't even realize it. For example:

- One slice of Costco's cheese pizza contains 1,370 milligrams of salt. That one slice of pizza almost contains almost your entire day's worth of sodium intake.
- There is more salt in a small chocolate milkshake (190 milligrams) than in a small order of McDonalds French fries (140 milligrams).
- Canned foods and prepackaged foods have higher salt content than fresh or frozen.

Watch out for the salt! Another interesting fact about salt is its ability to attract water. Salt makes us thirsty, requiring us to drink more water to

---

[21] *Wikipedia*, "Salt." Date of access: April 21, 2017 (https://en.wikipedia.org/wiki/Salt).

[22] *U.S. Food & Drug Administration*, "Lowering Salt in Your Diet." May 18, 2010 (https://www.fda.gov/ForConsumers/ConsumerUpdates/ucm181577.htm).

[23] *Centers for Disease Control and Prevention*, "Most Americans Should Consume Less Sodium." December 28, 2016 (https://www.cdc.gov/salt).

[24] Osagie K. Obasogie, *Slate*, "Black Salt: Should the Government Single Out African-Americans for Low-Sodium Diets?" April 18, 2011 (http://www.slate.com/articles/health_and_science/medical_examiner/2011/04/black_salt.html).

function properly. There is a normal relationship between salt and water to maintain a healthy balance in the body.

Are you living a balanced life that is both salty and watery? If yes, you should be attracting thirsty souls that need both your salt and watering from the Word of God in your life.

Take daily care of your temple (body), because you are the salt and light for the world.

> *Ye are the light of the world. A city that is set*
> *on an hill cannot be hid.*
> (Matthew 5:14).

The Lord wants you to be salty so that He can display Himself through your dedicated, disciplined, and well-managed life. Your life is much bigger than you; your commitment to stepping into the beauty of holiness is for His glory! He wants to show you off so that others will be inspired to live for Him, too. It's important for the physical body to manage your health through proper nutrition, exercise, and rest.

Reducing salt (sodium) consumption in your diet can naturally improve your physical health. To become spiritually healthy and salty, so that others are able to recognize that Christ lives in you, you will need to pray daily, study and learn God's Word, and worship corporately (fellowship with other believers on a regular basis). These three steps will improve your spiritual health and can cause you to become more beautiful both naturally and physically. Remember, you are a spirit, which has a soul, which lives in a body. Become a mature soul that can be used to season all!

Prayer Guide

Wow, Lord, I now realize how awesome You are. You actually created me to display Your ways and Your Word in my life. I love, appreciate, and respect You, and Your will for my life. You want me to live a life that will season all. I sincerely ask for Your help and guidance each and every day. Teach me, so that I can teach and inspire others. Lord, please also heal me physically and help me to discipline my life so that I will properly care for both my spiritual and physical body, and be a whole and healthy temple for Your glory. Amen!

Action Step

DAY TWENTY-FIVE

Sweet Sleeping Beauty

SCRIPTURE READING: PSALMS 4:1–8

MEMORY VERSE
When thou liest down, thou shalt not be afraid: yea,
thou shalt lie down, and thy sleep shall be sweet.
(Proverbs 3:24)

Now, I lay me down to sleep,
I pray the Lord my soul to keep.
His love to guard me through the night,
And wake me in the morning's light
(Addison, 1711)

Sixty percent of all American adults experience some form of regular sleep problems.[25] Sleep deprivation has negative effects on one's work performance and physical and mental health. It results in deduced energy, greater difficulty concentrating, and a diminished mood. A lack of sleep

---

[25] *National Sleep Foundation*, "How Much Sleep Do We Really Need?" Date of access: October 7, 2015 (https://sleepfoundation.org/excessivesleepiness/content/how-much-sleep-do-we-really-need-0).

also strains your relationships with God and others due to tiredness, fatigue, and irritability.

Lack of sleep is common in our society. How can we be effective examples of the beauty of holiness when we are physically and mentally exhausted? Our fast-paced lives cause us to overextend ourselves, stay up too late, and have poor nutrition because of grabbing fast food on the go and rushing through meals. Some learning and memory difficulties can be caused by not developing good sleep habits.

The Bible provides us guidance about how to be blessed with a sweet sleep:

Find your place in the Lord:
I will not give sleep to mine eyes, or slumber to mine
eyelids, until I find out a place for the Lord, an
habitation for the mighty God of Jacob.
(Psalm 132:4–5)

Labor in excellence:
The sleep of a labouring man is sweet, whether he eat
little or much: but the abundance of the rich will not
suffer him to sleep.
(Ecclesiastes 5:12)

Live in peace with God and man:
I will both lay me down in peace, and sleep: for
thou, Lord, only makest me dwell in safety.
(Psalm 4:8)

Follow these sleep practices on a consistent basis:

1. Establish a regular bedtime and wake schedule, even on the weekends.
2. Drink less fluids two hours before going to sleep.
3. Exercise regularly, but preferably before 7:00 p.m.
4. Consume less or no caffeine (especially after 2:00 p.m.) and avoid alcohol and nicotine.
5. Try a relaxing evening routine, like a hot bath and prayer before bedtime.

Upon this I awaked, and beheld;
and my sleep was sweet unto me
(Jeremiah 31:26).

Prayer Guide

Heavenly Father, the giver of all life, health, and sleep, I need Your sweet blessing over my life in order to carry out Your daily will through my life. Please guide me in the ways I should go, so that my life will not be overly stressful. Please forgive me when I cause my own life drama through fleshly desires, such as overcommitting myself, overextending myself, and mismanaging my recreation time. I have sometimes allowed myself to take time for myself instead of spending it with You. Create in me a clean heart and renew a right spirit within me (Psalm 51:10) so that I will develop a life that will be organized and honor my commitment to You first, in Jesus' name, Amen!

Action Step

DAY TWENTY-SIX

Style It Right!

Scripture Reading: Daniel 10:1–12

Memory Verse

…O man greatly beloved, fear not: peace be unto thee,
be strong, yea, be strong. And when he had spoken unto
me, I was strengthened, and said, Let my lord speak;
for thou hast strengthened me.
(Daniel 10:19)

During these thirty days of stepping into the beauty of holiness, you may have noticed that you also entered a season of strengthening. This may be a new style of garment for some of you, but it's time to style your life right by wearing the Word of God. Styling it right means wearing the living Word of God.

Strength is a foundational garment that you will learn to wear when you spend more time with the Lord. This is the first key. When He strengthens you, it affects every area of your life. Strength is defined as "the quality or state of being physically strong."[26] Strength is such a

---

[26] *Merriam-Webster*, "Strength." Date of access: April 21, 2017 (https://www.merriam-webster.com/dictionary/strength).

beautiful garment to wear. It attracts accessories such as increased divine favor, great grace, mercy, and peace over you and your family, even during storms and trials of life.

My prayer has been to empower you to grow and become a doer of God's Word, one who leads others toward Christ and the beauty of His holiness through your personal assessment and biblical application. If you spent little time in the presence of the Lord, you will receive little power, which could affect how you are spiritually dressed. Spending much time in the presence of the Lord equals greater power to do His will, and to be dressed for success!

In today's scripture reading, Daniel needed strength for the vision he obtained while he was alone (Daniel 10:1). The first key is that you need time alone with God so that He can give you vision, inspiration, and then strength for the task. Sin can rob you of your relationship with God, and therefore your strength. We were not created to carry the weight of sin, so handle sin quickly.

Here is the second key, and something to ponder about sin: many individuals, nations, and churches today have spiritual STDs (sin, transmitted death). Do not be a carrier or spreader of spiritual STDs. If you are spiritually sick, seek out help and counsel from qualified, mature, seasoned women of God in a position of proper authority. Spiritual sin can also make you physically sick, in which case you should seek a physician. Don't defraud yourself or others!

> To defraud is to excite physical or emotional desires that cannot be righteously fulfilled.[27]

---

[27] Jackie Kendall and Debby Jones, *Lady in Waiting: Becoming God's Best While Waiting for Mr. Right* (Shippensburg, PA: Destiny Image, 1997), 124.

Defrauding oneself will birth the Lord's correction in your life, so if and when you sin, repent, seek forgiveness, and turn from your wicked ways to restore a right relationship with the Lord.

> *That no man go beyond and defraud his brother in any*
> *matter: because that the Lord is the avenger of all such,*
> *as we also have forewarned you and testified.*
> (1 Thessalonians 4:6)

The next interesting fact about this passage of scripture is that Daniel lay himself before the Lord in prayer (Daniel 10:9), and then the Lord spoke His Word to Daniel, giving him strength.

The third key is that God's Word will never tell you to do something that will harm you or others. His Word can be trusted. Add trust and loyalty to your garment of strength, be faithful to yourself and others, and just be kind. So if it is not in the Word of God, don't do it and rebuke the enemy who is trying to get you to do something that will allow him legal access into your life. Sin gives the enemy access into our lives, so resist the devil and he will flee.

The final key from today's scripture is to *"fear not"* (Daniel 10:12). When God gives you a vision or mission, it is His responsibility to give you the strength to accomplish it. A fear-not garment is heavy to wear, but necessary to become bold, beautiful, and an effective woman of God. Pay close attention when God's Word says, "Fear not." This normally means that a big statement is about to be made, a big vision or mission, a big task or instruction. Big ideas, dreams, and visions require great faith, dedication, and strength from God. Your belief that God can do it through you activates the strength in you to do it.

Please note that God will train you by starting off with little tasks.

His lord said unto him, Well done, thou good and
faithful servant: thou hast been faithful over a few
things, I will make thee ruler over many things: enter
thou into the joy of thy lord.
(Matthew 25:21)

If you are humbly serving and faithful to your little assignments with joy, He will gradually increase them to bigger tasks. Style it right through the beauty of holiness, and become a classy, modest, elegant gracious DIVA (divinely inspired, victorious, anointed) woman of God!

Prayer Guide

Gracious God of all strength and comfort, I humbly ask You to clothe me right. I want to honor and be one who glorifies You through a life of righteous, holy living. I need You, Lord, and I want my life to project Your strength and divine favor. I love You, Jesus, and I want to be the divinely inspired DIVA woman of God! Prepare me daily to reach a soul each day. I am inspired by Your Word to grow in Your grace, Word, and knowledge. I will seek You with my whole heart, your DIVA daughter, in Jesus' name, Amen!

Action Step

DAY TWENTY-SEVEN

Can You Wait 'Til God Comes?

SCRIPTURE READING: ISAIAH 40:28–31

MEMORY VERSE

But they that wait upon the Lord shall renew their
strength; they shall mount up with wings as eagles;
they shall run, and not be weary;
and they shall walk, and not faint.
(Isaiah 40:31)

Waiting is one of the most complex yet basic principles of the Christian walk. Mastering the art of waiting can prove to be a valuable tool toward reaching maturity in God. If you are a mover and a shaker, or the one who makes things happen in the world of work, then having to wait on God can be an eye-opening experience. How do we wait? What do we do while we wait? And what do we learn from waiting?

I will try to shine some light on these three questions from my own personal valley experience on waiting on God. In year eighteen of my marriage, things began to grow worse over a five-year period, but ultimately I faced the devastation of being separated, divorced, and completely abandoned. For the next two years, many tears were shed, and many moments were spent asking God how and why this had happened to me. During the quiet moments of despair, and the aching pain of my broken heart, a wonderful relationship developed between me and the Lord through my healing process.

How do you wait? With joy. My circumstances were horrible, but I lived through them. I found great comfort in God's Word and the love of the saints. The Lord made me a Ruth. He had always taken care of me before, but it seemed that He was even better now than before the trial. I found myself praying more for my former husband than I ever had before he left, and I began to see him as a lost soul who again needed a Savior.

What do you do while you wait? The Word says, *"Occupy till I come"* (Luke 19:13). I began serving others more, participating in a divorce care/singles ministry group. By the way, I had a blast. I had never gone hiking on the side of a waterfall before for a Bible study, and it was awesome! My life took on a whole new meaning and I began to grow content in my new life. The Lord used me even more in my brokenness and singleness. I depended on Him for my dear life. My focus changed, I continued school, and I worked more on my health and fitness. I did things that brought beauty and joy back into my life.

Ask the Lord to direct you and your time, and please don't try to make things happen before His time. If you let God move in all of your waiting, you will find rest.

Come unto me, all ye that labour and are heavy laden,
and I will give you rest.
(Matthew 11:28)

Three years later, I was still waiting for God to move on my situation. I had become content in my singleness and began to reach out and minister again. You see, I felt that I had failed God, because my former husband had left. It took time for me to realize that I was still usable. And once I embraced how much God loved and valued me, my wholeness came, and then He reconciled me with my former husband for a season of another seven years.

Yes, I said three years later. When I was at peace in my life, and I was open to whatever the Lord had for me, He restored my marriage for another seven years.

Then, after thirty-one years, we finally ended our marriage and became friends who support our adult children. These new happily single years have been the better years of my life, and they are no comparison to the earlier years. I would have never thought I would be grateful that our marriage ended, but I don't miss it one bit. But I had to wait for my change to come. God's plan was really not pretty at all, and I must admit that it hurt an awful lot, but I wouldn't trade the end result for anything.

What did I learn from waiting? Waiting is hard, but it is necessary for our maturity. It's so funny how some of the most painful things in life can later be the most joyful things. I learned that God is worth the wait, and if you ask Him, He will wait with you. I learned that He loves me enough to help me wait on Him. I learned that I am not in control of my life, and I don't want to be. I learned that waiting builds character, grace, and favor in Him. I learned that you don't have to have the pieces together in your life to be used by God.

Sisters, please step into the beauty of holiness by learning the art of waiting. Wait for your own personal change to come. For those women who have experienced divorce, separation, or abandonment, your own personal waiting may have a different end; God's best for you is by His design.

Please know that God knows what is best for you. He can restore your marriage if that is His plan for you, but if He doesn't, it is because He has your best interests in mind. He will never give you something that will hurt you, and He will never give you something before its time.

For you make-it-happen women, please humble yourselves under the mighty hand of God and practice waiting for His changes in your life. Clear your mind of all your ideas and contingence plans of how you envision your answered prayer.

> *But they that wait upon the Lord shall renew their*
> *strength; they shall mount up with wings as eagles;*
> *they shall run, and not be weary;*
> *and they shall walk, and not faint.*
> (Isaiah 40:31)

He will give you the strength and grace to wait for your change and your promises in Him. I promise you that learning to wait is a lifelong process. If you wait with joy, even though your situation may not be joyous, your wait will be shorter.

Prayer Guide

Dear Lord, this sister has told me about her waiting on you and it was worth it. I have serious situations in my life right now, Lord. Please forgive me for trying to offer You my own plans of resolution. I surrender to You and give You all of my expectations, Lord. I want and need your guidance in my life. Open my eyes to Your will and my purpose in life. Give me the courage to move when You say move and wait when You say wait. Lord, please sit and wait with me and bless others who are waiting for You to show up in their lives as well. I love You, Lord, and today I am stepping into the beauty of holiness through patiently waiting on You! In Jesus' name, Amen!

Action Step

DAY TWENTY-SEVEN

Balancing You, the Spiritual Guide Pyramid

SCRIPTURE READING: PHILIPPIANS 2:1–12

MEMORY VERSE

I will greatly rejoice in the Lord, my soul shall be joyful
in my God; for he hath clothed me with the garments
of salvation, he hath covered me with the robe of
righteousness, as a bridegroom decketh himself
with ornaments, and as a bride adorneth
herself with her jewels.
(Isaiah 61:10)

Answering your calling to live a glorious and balanced life through Christ is an intentional choice, and you need to make it daily. Living for God is intentional. Spending time praying and studying God's Word is intentional! Choosing whom to serve this day is intentional!

You have made it through a month-long prayer and devotional season that focused on developing the beauty of holiness in your life. The next step is to continue to practice and grow in the living Word, and to become a daily doer of the Word. Share your own life lessons with others and spiritually dress yourself daily. Remember that dressing for success spiritually includes clothing oneself in:

- salvation and righteousness (Isaiah 61:10)
- humility (1 Peter 5:5)
- mercy and truth (Proverbs 3:3)
- the service of grace to others in truth (John 1:14)
- the beauty of holiness (1 Chronicles 16:29)

This is what Scripture means when it instructs us to work out our own salvation with fear.

> *Wherefore, my beloved, as ye have always obeyed, not as*
> *in my presence only, but now much more in my absence,*
> *work out your own salvation with fear and trembling.*
> (Philippians 2:12).

We must work on ourselves and our lives daily to perfect a life that honors, reveres, and pleases the Lord. This is how we demonstrate our love and appreciation for our Savior.

Through reflecting on building a more beautiful life through holiness, we examined how to build a solid spiritual foundation (see Appendix B). I hope you noticed that building a life in Christ is based on knowing and applying God's Word:

- Maintain a private devotional life—pray, praise, and study Gods Word (2 Timothy 2:15).
- Maintain an active corporate fellowship in your local church and serve in your community (Hebrews 10:25).
- Openly share your faith through becoming the living Word. This will automatically attract others to you (2 Corinthians 3:2).

- Worship and praise will produce the strength you will need for your journey (Nehemiah 8:10).
- Take care of your physical temple (body). Have fun, develop a health relationship and support systems, develop other interest and hobbies, and exercise and eat healthy (1 Timothy 4:8).

These simple steps will pay off big, so you will be in a better position to handle life's storms when they take place. You will be strengthened in advance. Praise your way through life, because truly the joy of the Lord is our strength!

To every reader who has joined me on this journey, thank you. This has been a labor of living out love. Writing this has been an enormous life-altering experience, but I am grateful that the Lord trusted me with this task. In closing, I have prayed for your faith that you will not fail. Our lives are not our own. We belong to God by choice. Become an instrument through which the Lord can live. Be kind and gracious. And finally, be beautiful through stepping into the beauty of holiness! Now, pass it on.

Prayer Guide

I am so thankful to have spent this time to develop a deeper and closer relationship with You, Lord. I feel closer to You. I am grateful for Your goodness, kindness, and love. I have grown to appreciate and understand that You have my best interests in mind, so I will work on trusting You more. Lord, You are great, You are holy, and You have provided great guidance and examples for living a prosperous life in You! I close this thirty-day devotional with Your Word: *"Now unto him that is able to keep you from falling, and to present you faultless before the presence of his glory with exceeding joy, to the only wise God our Saviour, be glory and majesty, dominion and power, both now and ever"* (Jude 24–25). In Jesus' precious name, Amen!

Action Step

DAY TWENTY-EIGHT

Reflection and Assignment

1. Scriptures Review:
Name one truth you have gained from each day.
- Exodus 12:1–28
- Matthew 5:1–12
- Psalms 4:1–8
- Daniel 10:1–12
- Philippians 2:1–12

2. Summarize one key truth from each devotionals lesson.

-
-
-
-
-

3. What is the most important behavioral change you will make regarding your mental and emotional health?

4. List one key prayer truth you have given to the Lord each day.

-
-
-
-
-

5. To whom or for what do you need to seek the Lord's forgiveness?

-
-
-
-
-

DAY TWENTY-NINE

Your Corporate Day of Worship

MEMORY VERSE

The glory of this latter house shall be greater than of the former, saith the Lord of hosts: and in this place will I give peace, saith the Lord of hosts.
(Haggai 2:9)

Closing Prayer

Lord, thank you for the opportunity to show You in praise and worship today how much I love and appreciate the growth and maturity that I have gain through stepping into the beauty of holiness journey. I am forever grateful in Jesus name, Amen!

DAY THIRTY

Review and Revisit Devotional Days

SET GOALS AND STRATEGIES TO MAINTAIN THE BEAUTY OF HOLINESS LIFESTYLE

I, _____ (name), commit to the following goals:

Goal #1: _____

Goal #2: _____

Goal #3: _____

Goal #4: _____

Goal #5: _____

Now that I have completed my thirty-day devotional journey toward stepping into the beauty of holiness, I will share my experience/testimony with five individuals:

Witness #1: _____

Witness #2: _____

Witness #3: _____

Witness #4: _____

Witness #5: _____

CONCLUSION

Enjoy the fresh fruit that the beauty of holiness will bring into your life. Examine and measure yourself, your heart, and your motives by God's standards from His Word often. Keep yourself clean, healed, and delivered through forgiveness.

Remember, as the saying goes, that we are not humans experiencing life as spiritual beings, but spiritual beings experiencing the human experience. Love truly lifted me!

Every job is a **self-portrait** of the person who does it. Autograph your work with **excellence** through becoming **extraordinary**!

APPENDIX A
THE AUTHOR'S PERSONAL TESTIMONY

THE BLESSING OF FORGIVENESS

I am a believer who has struggled with emotional hurt and pain through enabling, betrayal, abuse, anger, frustration, resentment, and insecurity.

As a child, I lived in a very abusive environment. My mom was an alcoholic. She numbed her pain and the depression of her own abuse. My father abused her, so in turn she abused me until I was sixteen. I was raised Catholic, but after being confirmed I left to attend a Holiness church, where I was saved at the age of twelve. I was a nervously outgoing child, but also lonely and sickly most of the time. I carried many family secrets that injured my emotions and my sense of self.

I served the Lord from the age of twelve to nineteen. I sang, taught Sunday school, became a junior missionary at sixteen, and excelled in school. Our family had improved, my mom joined AA, and she put me into a program for teens of parents who drink. I served the Lord faithfully until age nineteen, but then my disillusionment, disappointment, and an extremely difficult marriage resulted in me backsliding and leaving the Lord until I was twenty-five.

I was restored at Faith Assembly of Christ in Washington, where I faithful served for the next twenty-seven years. There I learned how much I missed being in fellowship with God, and I have never looked back. My problems, trials, sicknesses, and discouragements didn't end, but leaving the Lord was no longer an option for me.

These are the circumstances I experienced, which others might relate to:

1. Abuse (feeling helpless).
2. The pain of separation and divorce (feeling worthless).
3. Abandonment (feeling thrown away).
4. The loss of self-value and worth (feeling like I didn't deserve to be happy).
5. Being disrespected (wanting to be valued, to matter).
6. Suffering in silence (feeling ashamed).
7. Wanting desperately to be loved without pain (I tried to earn it).
8. Living in shame and embarrassment.

My Relationship with God

In spite of my personal suffering, I have been serving in a leadership role for more than twenty-seven years, and these have been both the best and sometimes worst times of my life.

I learned as a child to suffer in silence, which caused me not to seek professional help, because I was ashamed and embarrassed about still living and accepting abuse in my life as a pastor's wife. I coped through my academic and professional life, areas in which the Lord always blessed me and used as a means of restoring my self-esteem, value, and self-worth. I experienced so many blessings in other areas of my life that I just accepted that this was the way it was going to be.

My Attitude toward Others

Serving others through the years has been a blessing and healing. It has kept me from being consumed and self-absorbed. But sometimes the stuff in my private life has kept me nervous about letting people get too close.

I was always putting on a show, which caused me a lot of inner pressure. This was so very hard and painful. I remember praying and fasting the same prayer for over two years: "Lord, don't you see and don't you know? Please, Lord, help me!"

Well, one day He did help me. My marriage ended after eighteen years, and then I remarried him. It finally ended for good in 2010 after thirty-one years. Through the death of my marriage, the Lord healed me and made me whole. He kept me and made me a Ruth, a woman of God who has depended on the Lord for her very life.

I realized that even though I was able to forgive and move on, I was still afraid to address some of the issues that had ended my marriage. Not wanting to feel like a failure, and wanting to please the Lord and everyone around me, I suppressed many areas of concern that made me nervous and afraid inside.

What Was My Bottom?

I had a place inside where I hid my many wounds, but a situation happened that reminded me of all this past hurt. I found myself in such a state of rage that I wanted to hit the person who caused this situation. I mean, I really wanted to hurt them. This scared me! Because this was not normally my character, I went into Christian counseling, which led me to be open toward recovery.

Working Through the Celebrate Recovery Program

My oldest daughter had been asking me for months to come and sing with the church's praise team. I told her that recovery was her thing and I would support her, and maybe serve in the ministry, but I didn't need recovery for myself. Actually, I needed it badly.

My relationship with the Lord became more intimate. He has been closer to me than ever before. He gave me the courage to break the silence and expose the sin, and the enemy, that caused my shame and guilt. The Lord helped me identify the areas buried inside me that were causing my anger, leading me to accept the things I couldn't change.

Working through the program, it comes to mind that it was good that I was afflicted. It led me to a closer relationship with Christ. I came to understand what recovery is, and Jesus conducted a search-and-rescue mission to seek out a valuable treasure—me. He found me.

These are the seven stages of the healing process:

1. Denial and crying.
2. Recognizing enabling behaviors in myself and in my life.
3. Acknowledging my own powerlessness and the presence of controlling behaviors in my life, which arise from fear.
4. Repenting through purging and cleaning out my life.
5. Setting boundaries.
6. Speaking up for myself.
7. Forgiving again, and living again with purpose (Matthew 18:21–22).

The two most difficult steps for me were recognizing and facing my enabling behaviors, and acknowledging my own powerlessness.

Author Sharon Jaynes has defined forgiveness this way:

> To forgive means to no longer use the offense against the offender. It has nothing to do with whether or not the offender deserves forgiveness. Most do not, I do not deserve God's forgiveness, and yet He has forgiven me. Forgiving is taking someone off of your hook and

placing him or her on God's hook. It is the gift that you give yourself.[28]

It's more about what you do than what was done to you.

Choosing to move forward restored and renewed my hope, joy, and dreams. It has put my destiny back on course and opened up new areas of gifting and anointing inside me.

I had to acknowledge my own insecurities and recognize that we shouldn't have to earn other people's love. Not even Jesus's love can be earned, so having to make someone love you is not love.

THE NEW ME

Through the lessons I've learned from these experiences, I have grown to love the Lord more today than I did yesterday. I am so grateful for my life in the Lord and am forever grateful for my wholeness and the positive, fruitful suffering that has developed godly character within me. My life in Christ has grown more open and transparent, and I now live a lifestyle with which God would be pleased and of which I am not ashamed. I am moving fully into my purpose and destiny in life, without carrying past hurts and unforgiveness. It's priceless! Who I am in the Lord is what He has made me to be. Everything I do, no matter what the arena, I do to glorify the Lord in a spirit of excellence. My dependence, strength, faith, and hope are all in the Lord. To God be the glory for the great things He has done.

Even though the disastrous effects of my life took on many forms, such as my mother and my former husband, the real fact of the matter is that it was satan (I purposely don't capitalize the name). he comes to steal, kill, and destroy us—to deceive me. Jaynes has defined a deceiver as

---

[28] Sharon Jaynes, *The Ultimate Makeover: Becoming Spiritually Beautiful in Christ* (Chicago, IL: Moody Publishers, 2003), 144–145.

"someone who presents a lie in such a way that it sounds like the truth. He can make you believe something is not true when it is and make you believe that something is true when it isn't."[29] That is what the enemy tried to do to me: to rob me of my value, self-worth, and the promised abundant life in Christ Jesus.

Today I will continue to work on this vessel, through living an active life in the Lord. I have to continue to grow in the Lord and His knowledge, and also watch and pray so I can guard my heart, spirit, and emotions, which have been wounded and broken. I have to daily continue to trust Him since my sense of security and value was damaged. My dependence and expectations come from the Lord. My value and self-worth are now defined by what the Lord says about me, not by my past issues and drama. I am a royal priesthood, a holy nation, a beloved child, an heir, and a friend. How wonderful a Father He is to make me all those things.

As far as my healing, His presence and anointing keeps me alive daily. He gives me the grace to endure and overcome life's challenges as they come. My ability to release past hurts and the people who hurt me comes from God. My ability to recognize the deceiver as the enemy has enabled me to release others through the art of forgiveness. I am now able to obtain deliverance from a root of bitterness and unforgiveness (I self-examine often). The Lord enables me to forgive beyond my own human ability.

Living in Christ, for me, is a lifelong process which I have learned to take one day at a time, one moment at a time, even one second at a time. I live my life to inspire others to fall in love with Jesus. He is the answer for all of life's conditions and He lifted me up out of agony, despair, and regret. He said,

> But they that wait upon the Lord shall renew their
> strength; they shall mount up with wings as eagles;

---

[29] Ibid., 106.

*they shall run, and not be weary; and they
shall walk, and not faint.*
(Isaiah 40:31)

*Ye are our epistle written in our hearts,
known and read of all men...*
(2 Corinthians 3:2)

WHAT ENCOURAGEMENT CAN I GIVE A NEWCOMER?

Stay the course. It can be difficult to examine yourself and your motivations for doing things. Finding out what drives your behavior is the foundation for changing your behavior. It can be very uncomfortable, but it is necessary for God to use you.

Keep this journey about you personally and your issues, needs, and healing. You are not to try to fix anyone but yourself, and only that through God's guidance and help. Blaming and finding fault in others won't work. Be completely honest with yourself and those who have been assigned to help you. Cut your losses. Let go the past, so you can grab your future and move on, because your issues, gifts, and abilities will be used to help others overcome as well (Romans 8:28).

You are a unique treasure to God. He loves you very much and you are worth saving. He wants to recover and heal you back to the original that He intended you to be. Amen. When Christ looks at my self-portrait, He should be able to see a reflection of Himself. I will keep working on this until He comes!

Testimony Background Scriptures

*Then came Peter to him, and said, Lord, how oft shall
my brother sin against me, and I forgive him? till seven
times? Jesus saith unto him, I say not unto thee, Until
seven times: but, Until seventy times seven.*
(Matthew 18:21–22)

*And we know that all things work together for good to
them that love God, to them who are the called according
to his purpose.*
(Romans 8:28)

*Therefore if any man be in Christ, he is a new creature:
old things are passed away; behold, all things are become
new. And all things are of God, who hath reconciled
us to himself by Jesus Christ, and hath given to us the
ministry of reconciliation; To wit, that God was in
Christ, reconciling the world unto himself, not imputing
their trespasses unto them; and hath committed unto us
the word of reconciliation. Now then we are ambassadors
for Christ, as though God did beseech you by us: we pray
you in Christ's stead, be ye reconciled to God. For he hath
made him to be sin for us, who knew no sin; that we
might be made the righteousness of God in him.*
(2 Corinthians 5:17–21)

*But ye are a chosen generation, a royal priesthood, an
holy nation, a peculiar people; that ye should shew forth
the praises of him who hath called you out of darkness*

*into his marvellous light; which in time past were not a
people, but are now the people of God: which had not
obtained mercy, but now have obtained mercy.*
(1 Peter 2:9)

APPENDIX B
THE SPIRITUAL GUIDE PYRAMID

The spiritual guide pyramid concept is based on the food guide pyramid concept and is my original idea.[30]

THE FOUNDATIONAL LIFE

*Oh that men would praise the Lord for his goodness, and
for his wonderful works to the children of men!*
(Psalm 107:8)

*Praise ye the Lord: for it is good to sing praises unto our
God; for it is pleasant; and praise is comely.*
(Psalm 147:1)

*I will sing of the mercies of the Lord forever: with
my mouth will I make known thy faithfulness to all
generations.*
(Psalm 89:1)

---

[30] U.S. Department of Agriculture, *The Food Guide Pyramid*. Revised October 1996 (https://www.cnpp.usda.gov/sites/default/files/archived_projects/FGPPamphlet.pdf).

THE SPIRITUAL LIFE GUIDE PYRAMID

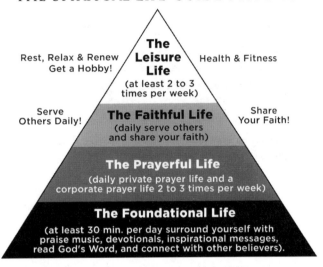

Enjoying a combination of at least 6 to 12 servings per week from each one of the 4 life areas will ensure a **EXCELLENT** FRUITFUL LIFE!

THE FOUNDATIONAL LIFE[31] [32]

But the hour cometh, and now is, when the true worshippers shall worship the Father in spirit and in truth: for the Father seeketh such to worship him.
(John 4:23)

God is a Spirit: and they that worship him must worship him in spirit and in truth.
(John 4:24)

[31] Carroll, J. (2017). What is the meaning of Christian worship?" Retrieved August 25, 2017 from https://www.gotquestions.org/Christian-worship.html

[32] Shotlow, D. (2013). "Worship Foundations." Retrieved August 25, 2017 from http://www.experiencingworship.com/worship-articles/general/2002-8-Worship-Foundations--p11.html

THE PRAYERFUL LIFE[33]

Pray without ceasing.
(1 Thessalonians 5:17)

*Call unto me, and I will answer thee, and show thee
great and mighty things, which thou knowest not.*
(Jeremiah 33:3)

THE FAITHFUL LIFE[34] [35]

Thou shalt have no other gods before me.
(Exodus 20:3)

*Not forsaking the assembling of ourselves together, as the
manner of some is; but exhorting one another: and so
much the more, as ye see the day approaching.*
(Hebrews 10:25)

*A faithful man shall abound with blessings: but he that
maketh haste to be rich shall not be innocent.*
(Proverbs 28:20)

---

[33] *Got Questions?* "Why Is Daily Prayer Important?" Date of access: May 29, 2017 (https://www.gotquestions.org/daily-prayer.html).

[34] *All About…*, "Faithfulness to God." Date of access: May 29, 2017 (http://www.allaboutgod.com/faithfulness-to-god-faq.htm).

[35] *Pastors.com*, "7 Ways God Will Evaluate Your Faithfulness." Date of access: May 29, 2017 (http://pastors.com/7-ways-god-will-evaluate-faithfulness/).

THE LEISURE LIFE[36] [37] [38]

Let us labour therefore to enter into that rest, lest any
man fall after the same example of unbelief.
(Hebrews 4:11)

---

[36] Workout recommendations: *American Heart Association*, "American Heart Association Recommendations for Physical Activity in Adults." July 27, 2016 (http://www.heart.org/HEARTORG/HealthyLiving/PhysicalActivity/FitnessBasics/American-Heart-Association-Recommendations-for-Physical-Activity-in-Adults_UCM_307976_Article.jsp#.WSxSUWjyu01).

[37] Get a hobby: Marlen Komar, *Bustle*, "How to Find a Hobby as an Adult." October 29, 2015 (https://www.bustle.com/articles/119942-how-to-find-a-hobby-as-an-adult).

[38] Rest, relax, renew: Dr. Karin Luise, *Huffington Post*, "How to Relax and Renew Yourself Right This Moment." April 29, 2014 (http://www.huffingtonpost.com/dr-karin-l-smithson/how-to-relax-and-renew-yo_b_4861695.html).

DEFINITIONS OF GUIDING TERMS:

Word	Meaning
Beauty	(a) Beauty is "a characteristic of an animal, idea, object, person or place that provides a perceptual experience of pleasure or satisfaction."[4] (b) "The experience of 'beauty' often involves an interpretation of some entity as being in balance and harmony with nature, which may lead to feelings of attraction and emotional well-being."[5] (c) "Aristotle saw a relationship between the beautiful (*to kalon*) and virtue, arguing that 'Virtue aims at the beautiful.'"[6] (d) "The characterization of a person as 'beautiful', whether on an individual basis or by community consensus, is often based on some combination of *inner beauty*, which includes psychological factors such as personality, intelligence, grace, politeness, charisma, integrity, congruence and elegance, and *outer beauty* (i.e. physical attractiveness) which includes physical attributes which are valued on an aesthetic basis."[7]

Bitterness	"Bitterness has a tenacious way of taking root deep within the soul and resisting all efforts to weed it out. The results of unforgiveness is developing a root of bitterness."[8]
Forgiveness	(a) "To forgive means to no longer use the offense against the offender. It has nothing to do with whether or not the offender deserves forgiveness. Most do not, I do not deserve God's forgiveness, and yet He has forgiven me. Forgiving is taking someone off of your hook and placing him or her on God's hook. It is the gift that you give yourself."[9] (b) "Forgiveness is the intentional and voluntary process by which a victim undergoes a change in feelings and attitude regarding an offense, lets go of negative emotions such as vengefulness, with an increased ability to wish the offender well."[10] (c) "Forgiveness is ultimately a gift to yourself. It allows the wounds to heal."[11]

Holiness	(a) "Holiness—His holy nature—is progressively going to fill my broken, weak and damaged parts. The character and constancy of my Father will grow in me." [12] (b) "We understand the word generally to mean 'divine' or 'of God.'" [13] (c) "That's what 'holiness' is really about—wholeness. What the Holy Spirit is up to is bringing the *whole* life of Jesus Christ into the *whole* of our personalities so that the *whole* love of God can be relayed to the *whole* world." [14] (d) "…Holiness/sanctification involves your *peace, completeness and wholeness…* In short, God is ready to do everything He can to put you fully together, starting today! Paul's prayer holds a tremendous promise: 'May the God of peace… sanctify you.' The essential idea of the word *eirene* (peace) is unity, of fragments or separated parts being brought together. This is a wonderful promise, relevant to our own broken hearts." [15]

Holy	(a) "For I am the Lord your God: ye shall therefore sanctify yourselves, and ye shall be holy; for I am holy…" (Leviticus 11:44) (b) "…our holiness has been secured before God by virtue of our position in Jesus Christ. Jesus' sinless record was credited to your account."[16] (c) "The English word "holy" dates back to at least the 11th century with the Old English word *hālig*, an adjective derived from *hāl* meaning 'whole' and used to mean 'uninjured, sound, healthy, entire, complete'."[17]
Offense	"The Greek word for 'offend' in Luke 17:1 comes from the word *skandalon*. This word originally referred to the part of the trap to which the bait was attached. Hence the word signifies laying a trap in someone's way. In the New Testament it often describes an entrapment used by the enemy."[18]

Sacred	(a) First used in the fourteenth century, sacred means "revered due to sanctity and is general the state of being perceived by religious individuals as associated with divinity and considered worthy of spiritual respect or devotion; or inspiring awe or reverence among believers."[19] (b) Sacred means "dedicated or set apart for the service or worship of a deity… highly valued and important… deserving to be respected and honored."[20] (d) Sacred, from the Greek word *hagion*, means "in a moral sense, pure, sinless, upright, holy."[21]
Unforgiveness	"Unforgiveness is a trap, a net and a snare. It will trap you like a fly in a spider web, it will suck the very life from your soul."[22]

Upcoming Books from Jacqueline M. Pressey

Beautifully Marred
This sequel to *Step into the Beauty of Holiness* is a 30 day devotional that will guide you through profiting from the pains in your life. Your scars and weaknesses can be made beautiful when placed in the Master's hands as He makes something new out of you for His glory.

The Battle Diet
Living purposefully by pursuing scripture-based
wholeness strategies and the spiritual
methods of examining one's
mind, body, soul,
and spirit.

FOOTNOTES

1 *Hebrew4Christians.com*, "Unleavened Bread." Date of access: May 26, 2017 (http://www.hebrew4christianscom/Holidays/Spring_Holidays/Unleavened_Bread/Anavah/anavah.html)

2 *Natural Food Benefits*, "Benefits of Lamb." Date of access: May 26, 2017 (http://www.naturalfoodbenefits.com/list-details.phpCAT=3&ID=104)

3 *Chabad.org*, "Maror: Eating the Bitter Herbs." Date of access: May 26, 2017 (http://www.chabad.org/holidays/passover/pesach_cdo/aid/2878334/jewish/Maror-Eating-the-Bitter-Herbs.htm)

4 *Wikipedia*, "Beauty." Date of access: May 15, 2017 (https://en.wikipedia.org/wiki/Beauty).

5 Ibid.

6 Ibid.

7 Ibid.

8 Sharon Jaynes, *The Ultimate Makeover: Becoming Spiritually Beautiful in Christ* (Chicago, IL: Moody Publishers, 2003), 144.

9 Ibid., 144–145.

10 *Wikipedia*, "Forgiveness." Date of access: May 15, 2017 (https://en.wikipedia.org/wiki/Forgiveness).

11 Mark Banschick, MD, *Psychology Today*, "Can You Forgive?" October 3, 2011 (https://www.psychologytoday.com/blog/the-intelligent-divorce/201110/can-you-forgive).

12 Jack Hayford, *Charisma Magazine*, "Jack Hayford Explains What Holiness Really Is." August 26, 2015 (http://www.charismamag.com/spirit/spiritual-growth/14575-wholly-holy).

13 Ibid.

14 Ibid.

15 Ibid.

16 Ibid.

17 *Wikipedia*, "Sacred." Date of access: May 15, 2017 (https://en.wikipedia.org/wiki/Sacred).

18 John Bevere, *The Bait of Satan: Living Free from the Deadly Trap of Offense* (Lake Mary, FL: Strang Communications, 1994), 7. Revised edition, 2004.

19 *Wikipedia*, "Sacred." Date of access: May 15, 2017 (https://en.wikipedia.org/wiki/Sacred).

20 *Merriam-Webster*, "Sacred." Date of access: May 15, 2017 (https://www.merriam-webster.com/dictionary/sacred).

21 *Thayer's Greek Lexicon*, "39. Hagion." Date of access: May 15, 2017 (https://www.merriam-webster.com/dictionary/sacred).

22 Sharon Jaynes, *The Ultimate Makeover: Becoming Spiritually Beautiful in Christ* (Chicago, IL: Moody Publishers, 2003), 143.